Thomas's America

Earl Ofari Hutchinson

Middle Passage Press
Los Angeles, CA

Publishers' Cataloging in Publication

Names: Hutchinson, Earl Ofari.
Title: Thomas's America / Earl Ofari Hutchinson.
Description: Los Angeles, CA : Middle Passage Press, 2023. |
    Includes bibliographic references and index. | Summary:
    Presents a revealing and critical look at Supreme Court
    Justice Clarence Thomas, who has been a major flashpoint of
    controversy on and off the court for more than three decades.
Identifiers: LCCN 2023912486 | ISBN 9799891211735
Subjects: LCSH: Thomas, Clarence, 1948- . | United States.
    Supreme Court. | Political questions and judicial power –
    United States. | Misconduct in office – United States. |
    Constitutional law – United States. | United States – Politics
    and government. | BISAC: POLITICAL SCIENCE / Ameri-
    can Government / Judicial Branch. | POLITICAL SCIENCE /
    Commentary & Opinion. | POLITICAL SCIENCE / Corrup-
    tion & Misconduct.
Classification: LCC KF8748 H88 2023 | DDC 347.73 H--dc23
LC record available at https://lccn.loc.gov/2023912486

Table of Contents

Introduction

"To define each of us by our race is nothing short of a denial of our humanity."

The supreme irony about Supreme Court of the United States (SCOTUS) Associate Justice Clarence Thomas is that he got on the Supreme Court because he was Black. He was in essence an affirmative action appointee. It happened this way. In June 1991, liberal Black SCOTUS Justice and civil rights icon Thurgood Marshall informed then-President George H.W. Bush, that he was retiring from the court.

Bush would nominate his successor. However, he was concerned about appearance. He quipped, "It looks like I'm putting a black in for a black." But this was disingenuous. There was little doubt that that was exactly what Bush intended to do. The pick of Thomas because of his color was glaringly obvious, particularly given Thomas's lackluster and thoroughly undistinguished stint as a federal appeals court judge. Bush later admitted that he had considered only one other possible court pick besides Thomas.

Now fast forward almost exactly thirty-two years later to June 2023. Thomas now had the distinction of being one of the longest-serving Justices in the history of the High Court—and he was livid. On June 30, 2023, the SCOTUS by a 6 to 3 vote had in effect sounded the final death knell for the use of any affirmative action race-based factors in college admissions.

Thomas, the man who was nominated for the High Court because he was Black, a naked racial preference, wasn't satisfied with that. He aimed his fire at fellow SCOTUS Justice, the liberal Ketanji Brown Jackson, who dared chastise him for his vote to toss affirmative action.

"As she sees things, we are all inexorably trapped in a fundamentally racist society, with the original sin of slavery and the historical subjugation of black Americans still determining our lives today. The panacea, she counsels, is to unquestioningly accede to the view of elite experts and reallocate society's riches by racial means as necessary to 'level the playing field,' all as judged by racial metrics. I strongly disagree."

*****

That was putting it mildly. Thomas's vehement and long-standing opposition to affirmative action since taking his seat on the high court in 1991 was the stuff of legend. He was repeatedly raked over the coals by liberals, many Democrats, and especially civil rights groups in the years before the SCOTUS's 2023 affirmative action decision.

The big rap against him was he was an arch-hypocrite. He was arguably a prime beneficiary of affirmative action programs, yet relentlessly opposed them. He was never shy in espousing his loathing for them and then doing everything he could to undermine and ultimately eliminate them.

Thomas survived one of the most brutal Senate confirmation grillings in court history in 1991. He was pilloried for everything from his thin legal experience to alleged incompetence on the bench. But what made daily headline news was the charge against him by Anita Hill of sexual harassment. The 52 to 48 Senate vote to confirm him was one of the closest in the history of court nominee confirmations.

Thomas did not forgive or forget the political mauling he got from labor, women, civil rights, and civil liberty groups, and from liberal Democrats. He vowed revenge.

Thomas was as good as his word. By 2023 he had been on the SCOTUS for thirty-plus years. During that time, his rulings on everything from corporate power, environmental regulations, abortion, gay rights and, most importantly, civil rights were the most consistent, unyielding, doctrinaire rightist opinions and dissents in court history.

*****

In *Thomas's America*, political analyst Earl Ofari Hutchinson brings to bear his extensive writings and analysis of SCOTUS Justice Clarence Thomas during Thomas's decades on the high court. He assesses the Thomas phenomena and its impact on law, public policy, and race in America.

He examines the controversies that have swirled around Thomas from his ultra-conservative political and ideological rigidity to charges of ethical and financial improprieties, as well as his borderline-legal cozying up with rightist billionaire backers. He presents a frightening view of how Thomas would reshape America as a power broker on the SCOTUS.

Thomas's America presents a revealing and critical, but always fascinating, look at a high court Justice—the Justice who has been a major flashpoint of controversy on and off the court for more than three decades.

1

Above the Law

"A judge should be evaluated by whether he faithfully upholds his oath to God, not to the people, to the state or the Constitution."

Clarence Thomas was adamant that "this sort of personal hospitality from close personal friends, who did not have business before the Court, was not reportable." This was the crux of the brief statement that the Justice issued in April 2023, in response to the intense heat that he was getting.

He was attacked by watchdog groups, many Democrats, and much of the media about his years of receiving lucrative financial favors, paying for expensive foreign jaunts on private planes and yachts, and staying at a luxurious vacation retreat. All were paid for by a Texas rightist billionaire GOP donor, Harlan Crow. Thomas brushed aside accusations of any impropriety.

He also brushed aside federal law. It clearly states that federal judges, and that includes Supreme Court Justices, are required to disclose such gifts and transactions under the Ethics in Government Act, which establishes rules for federal officials regarding what's acceptable. As detailed by the law, any transportation, gifts, and most real estate sales above $1,000 need to be disclosed.

This was more than a simple matter of one Justice skirting the disclosure law on financial transactions. Thomas's decision not to disclose his financial dealings, at least not immediately, was crucial to the schedule of cases that were coming before the Supreme Court in 2023. It was a matter of timing. Thomas asked and got an extension to disclose the financial favors in June 2023.

The date was particularly significant. The filing would not be completed and made public until after the Supreme Court ended its 2023 term on June 30, 2023. By then the court would have ruled on some of the most highly contested issues such as student loan forgiveness, which involved lending and the banks, and affirmative action, which involved racial privilege, and LGBT rights.

These were ever-present issues that conservatives, and the GOP, waged ferocious battles against. Thomas's billionaire patron Crow may not have had a direct personal stake in Thomas's decision on any of these issues. However, they were passionate issues for ultra-conservatives. Thomas's vote on them was predictable and hewed to the ultra-conservative stance. That would have been completely in line with Crow's views. Crow vehemently denied that he had spoken with Thomas about any case or matter before the court. But he didn't have to.

*****

For his part, Crow could almost have come from a Hollywood casting agency for ultra-conservatives. He was a real estate magnate and a major donor to Republican organizations, among which were the Club for Growth and the Federalist Society. He was a board member of the American Enterprise Institute and the Hoover Institution. He donated hundreds of thousands of dollars to a Tea Party organization which just happened to have been founded by Thomas's wife, Virginia "Ginni" Thomas.

Thomas had one more ace to play in avoiding any charge of wrongdoing and to head off possible charges of ethics violations in his refusal to disclose. He cited the exemption loophole under the disclosure law that excludes some gifts judges receive under the label "personal hospitality." The exemption states that gifts of food, lodging, or entertainment received as "personal hospitality" don't have to be disclosed. However, it clearly states that gifts must be received at that person's home or at properties that they or their family own.

ProPublica, the financial watchdog group that dug up the disclosure rule violation by Thomas, polled more than a half dozen legal experts on ethics and disclosure laws. Not one of them saw anything in the exemption provision that applied to the massive amount of financial booty Thomas received and did not disclose.

Richard Painter, who served as the chief ethics lawyer for the George W. Bush White House, said Thomas's explanation of why he didn't disclose the trips "makes absolutely no sense." Painter emphasized that the exemption only covers three categories: food, lodging, and entertainment. Private jet flights would fall into none of those, he said.

Thomas remained defiant and still maintained that the gifts he received did fall under the exemption clause: "Early in my tenure at the Court, I sought guidance from my colleagues and others in the judiciary and was advised that this sort of personal hospitality from close personal friends, who did not have business before the Court, was not reportable." He did not name the "colleagues in the judiciary" who gave him this erroneous advice.

There may be another reason Thomas refuses to fully disclose the outside income he routinely receives. He ranks at the bottom among the SCOTUS Justices in terms of their financial worth. Thomas's official net worth is a relative paltry one million dollars. Beyond his SCOTUS salary, the scant financial disclosure made public by the Justices showed that Thomas has few other major investment assets. The outside perks Thomas got and remained silent about provided a major boost to his income and afforded him a relatively lavish lifestyle that he would have no chance to attain just on his income and assets alone.

*****

When the story about Crow's financial largesse to Thomas broke in April 2023, the obvious question was what could or would be done to hold Thomas accountable for his non-disclosure, which breached ethics violations. The answer was not reassuring. Apart from outrage and demands for an investigation by some Democrats, there was no move to act.

The Justice Department could have chosen to bring ethics violations charges against Thomas. However, there was no indication that it would act. The SCOTUS essentially was left to police itself when it came to ethics violations, a Justice's failure or refusal to disclose, and naked profiteering and influence peddling from outsiders. But what action it would take, if any, was at best limited, sketchy, and deliberately hazy. "The Supreme Court doesn't have any formal process for ensuring the justices comply with ethics rules," said Kedric Payne, the senior director of ethics at the Campaign Legal Center.

Some Democrats did attempt to hold Thomas and other judges who profited from their stint on the courts accountable. That meant closing the disclosure loopholes. They introduced several bills that would tighten the reins on the judges when it came to ethics and disclosure. However, along with the half-hearted calls for a Thomas investigation, the bills would likely go nowhere. Thomas, for all practical purposes, was home-free when it came to being required to make full and timely disclosure of any financial perks he got from outside sources.

Thomas's blatant thumbing of his nose at the law, ethics, and his profiteering, simply added to his well-earned reputation as a Justice who would be the paramount defender of the hard-core ultra-conservative realm on the bench—and one who also found a way above and beyond his relatively meager personal assets to profit handsomely from it.

2

Mr. "Originalist"

"And I don't think that government has a role in telling people how to live their lives. Maybe a minister does, maybe your belief in God does, maybe there's another set of moral codes, but I don't think the government has a role."

In November 2017, Thomas made what for him was the rarest of rarities: he granted a sit-down interview. For him, the venue and the host he chose for it was an easy call. It was on the stalwart news Bible of conservatives, the Fox News Network. The host was Laura Ingraham, the long-time outspoken media conservative pundit. Thomas also did something else relatively rare for him: he talked about his judicial philosophy. Ingraham gave him the cue when she described it as "alternatively formalistic, rigid, strictly conservative."

"I think it's get it right," Thomas said. "I think we are required to reason to a conclusion. That's what we try to do."

That of course didn't say, let alone tell, very much. However, as has been the case through nearly all of Thomas's decades on the Supreme Court, it was left to others to flesh out just exactly what that philosophy is, or as he put it, "get it right." The easy way is to simply say that he's a strict constructionist. That requires that he think a law and public policy decision must be made with a firm glance over his legal shoulder at what the Founding Fathers meant and wanted for the country in their framing of the Constitution.

The other term that some slap on this conservative legal and judicial reading is "originalism." That's adherence to the strict letter of the Constitution no matter that it was written in the eighteenth century and that time doesn't stand still. Things change; circumstances, conditions, and people change and evolve with the passage of time. Yet no matter what, the Constitution is what it is and must be strictly applied as judges such as Thomas maintain.

*****

A bevy of constitutional and legal scholars for decades have debated, sparred over, and interpreted what strict Constitutional construction meant and how it could and should be applied to court cases and decisions. But even on this, there has been much debate. One centers around the term "original intent" or trying to parse what the Founding Fathers meant and wanted. In one oft-cited case in 1905, *South Carolina v. United States*, it was stated, "The Constitution is a written instrument. As such its meaning does not alter. That which it meant when adopted, it means now."

In another case in 1934, *Home Bldg. & Loan Assn v. Blaisdell*, the court rejected without apology the idea that "the great clauses of the Constitution must be confined to the interpretation which the framers, with the conditions and outlook of their time, would have placed upon them." These were two court decisions, two separate and distinct views about what "original intent" meant and how rigid it should be adhered to.

Thomas, though, had no qualms about accepting the strict adherence view. In a dissent in one case in which he opposed the majority opinion, he explained, "the Court's holding is not supported by the original meaning . . . or any reasonable interpretation of our precedents."

Two compelling issues that Thomas had a golden opportunity to apply his "originalist" concept to were abortion and affirmative action. In both cases, Thomas took the position that there was no Constitutional provision or intent that abortion or a racial preference or even distinction were "rights."

The issue of what and how federal power can be used to legislate also was a major attack point for Thomas's originalist view in deciding court cases. This was plainly evident in Thomas's restrictive notion of how the interstate commerce clause should be, or rather not be, applied. In the pivotal 1995 case, *United States v. Lopez*, Thomas claimed that there was absolutely nothing in the Constitution that permitted Congress to regulate interstate commerce when it came to enacting laws that concerned "productive activities such as manufacturing and agriculture."

One had to scratch their head and ask, if that were the case, what exactly is the point of an interstate commerce clause if it has no power to regulate "productive" commerce? The logical but very problematic implication of this originalist view and application is that a law such as one that prohibits child labor that has been encoded in law and public policy for decades could be struck down. Why? Because there is nothing in the Constitution that specifically prohibits employers from utilizing child laborers.

*****

The major battle over greater environmental regulations was yet another area where Thomas's originalist notion posed a major danger. In a 2015 case, *Department of Transportation v. Association of American Railroads*, Thomas again applied his originalist standard. He flatly held that the Environmental Protection Agency should have no power to regulate energy, gas, oil, or other environmental polluters. His rationale was that they had no businesses or authority to "create generally applicable rules of private conduct."

Thomas was in effect saying that public agencies, particularly regulatory governmental agencies such as the EPA, could do nothing to institute and enforce safeguards for the environment and, by extension, the public. There would be no Clean Air Act or Clean Water Act or for that matter any other regulatory agency or regulations to protect the environment in his view. He would in effect give free rein to the energy industry to operate any way it saw fit, no matter how damaging to the environment and the health of the public.

Thomas came dangerously close to intimating he'd get rid of the Clean Water Act if he could. In his opinion backing the court's majority ruling that hamstrung the Act in an Idaho case in May 2023, Thomas left no doubt what the fate of the Act would be if it came to eliminating it, "The Court's opinion today curbs a serious expansion of federal authority that has simultaneously degraded States' authority and diverted the Federal Government from its important role as guarantor of the Nation's great commercial water highways into something resembling a local zoning board. But wetlands are just the beginning of the problems raised by the agencies' assertion of jurisdiction in this case." His pointed reference to the "beginning of the problems" with the Act left no doubt about how he viewed it.

*****

During Thomas's three-plus decades on the Supreme Court, he has also had to rule on numerous controversial criminal justice cases that involved the death penalty, police misconduct, search and seizure laws, jury racial bias, and the right to legal representation.

One case illustrates Thomas's originalist hard line, unbending standard. That came in a case that partially revisited the landmark 1963 case *Gideon v. Wainwright*. The court held in that case that criminal suspects have the right to counsel and that states are obliged to ensure that they do, by providing counsel if they can't pay for one themselves.

The Sixth Amendment, however, does not explicitly say that a defendant must have the right to counsel. Thomas took that fine distinction and ran with it. In the case in question, Luis in March 2016, Thomas based his Sixth Amendment reading on *Betts v. Brady*.

The Sixth Amendment, Thomas claimed, "abolished the rule prohibiting representation in felony cases," but was "not aimed to compel the State to provide counsel for a defendant." Thomas didn't say it directly, but the glaring implication was that there was no direct mandate in the Sixth Amendment for the state to provide counsel to an indigent person. Even more brutal, without that right and the assistance of state-supplied counsel, a defendant could be routinely imprisoned without ever receiving a word of advice, let alone representation from an attorney.

Thomas in this case, as in others, was if nothing else consistent. He was dutybound to uphold what he considered the original intent as he interpreted it of the Founding Fathers in writing the Constitution. No matter how out of date, inappropriate, or just plain ridiculous it is to apply hard and fast legal precepts with not the slightest room for interpretation from a document more than two centuries back to the twenty-first century's changed conditions.

That's less important to Thomas than that he remains one of the Supreme Court's foremost originalists. That requires that he purport to interpret the Constitution just as the Founders understood it in 1789.

3

More Than His Grandfather's Son

"My grandfather was a man when he talked about freedom, his attitude was really interesting. His view was that you had obligations, or you had responsibilities, and when you fulfilled those obligations or responsibilities, that then gave you the liberty to do other things.

A little more than a year after his 1991 bruising Supreme Court confirmation battle, a media gun-shy Clarence Thomas made his first cautious public appearance. He wanted the friendliest of friendly audiences for his public emergence.

He chose Mercer University, a conservative law school in Georgia for his speech. In his talk, Thomas got right to what he wanted to say, or more particularly, whom he wanted to lambaste. He cloaked himself in the martyr's garment and said that he expected to be treated badly by Blacks for daring to challenge the tenets of racial orthodoxy. "You were considered a traitor to your race, and not considered a real black person."

In 2023, a decade and a half afterward, Thomas hadn't budged one inch from his relentless public and private war against civil rights leaders and liberal Democrats. In his 2007 memoir, *My Grandfather's Son*, his war of ideology and words against them showed no signs of abating. He wrapped himself just as tightly in the martyr's garment as he did in his Mercer speech. He sledgehammered liberal Democrats and civil rights groups just as hard as before.

In the decades he's been on the bench and in the public light, many have tried to make sense of Thomas' doctrinaire, contrarian court votes and opinions, not to mention his unrelenting private war against civil rights groups. One explanation frequently offered is that they are payback to civil rights and civil liberties groups for trying to wreck his confirmation to the Supreme Court in 1991.

But there's more to it than that. For the thin-skinned Thomas, race has always lurked close to the surface—often too close. And it's intimately, but falsely, intertwined with the debate over conservative ideology.

*****

In the Mercer speech, and anyplace else where he's gotten the chance, Thomas has repeatedly bristled at the knock that civil rights leaders don't consider him a real Black person because of his ultra-conservative views. He railed at that and them in his Mercer speech, but for far different reasons than his Black critics say.

Many Blacks expect whites to espouse conservative views. That expectation is deeply colored by race. They can't separate racism from conservatism. Since many Blacks view whites as racist or as having racist views, they believe that conservatism must be a natural outgrowth of their incessant racial bigotry.

But racism and conservatism can be mutually incompatible. There is no one-to-one correlation between a conservative's espousal of free market economics and their attack on government regulations and them being a racial bigot. Yet the notion that a conservative is by definition a racist is deeply ingrained in the beliefs of many Blacks.

An October 2020 poll by the Public Religion Research Institute, seemed to confirm the jaundiced view that Republicans are almost always by that definition bigots. It found that the vast majority of them are rabid Fox News watchers and think that Blacks protest too much about racism. The topper was that many of them said that whites not Blacks are the target of "a lot of discrimination."

Thomas was not totally unmindful of how racist many Blacks regard conservatives as being. He has occasionally warned Republicans about racial insensitivity. And there are many Blacks whose views are just as conservative as his in opposing abortion and gay rights and affirmative action, and are just as hard-edged on crime and punishment.

It matters not. Thomas couldn't win. Civil rights leaders would never cease branding him as a fake, inauthentic Black man. He's the Black guy who sold his soul for a few pieces of conservative and even racist silver. A softball *60 Minutes* profile on him in September 2012 infuriated Thomas bashers. They were especially furious that the interviewer, Steve Kroft, let Thomas assail Anita Hill unchallenged. Kroft first played Thomas's angry rebuttal of Hill's allegations of sexual misconduct that she leveled against him at his confirmation hearing. Here's a snippet from the exchange with Thomas on Hill:

THOMAS [video clip]: This is a circus. It's a national disgrace. It is a high-tech lynching for uppity blacks who in any way deign to think for themselves. And it is a message that unless you kowtow to an old order, you will be lynched, destroyed, and caricatured by a committee of the U.S. Senate rather than hung from a tree.

KROFT: Why did you use that language? And why a "high-tech lynching"?

THOMAS: If somebody just wantonly tries to destroy you, if somebody comes in and just drags you out of your house and beats the hell out of you, what is it?

KROFT: What do you want people to think about those allegations? What's it—what is it important for people to think?

THOMAS: I—really, at this point, I think most well-meaning people understand it for what it was. It was a weapon to destroy me, clear and simple.

Thomas's critics were appalled at the softball questions to him, especially about Hill. CNN legal analyst Jeffrey Toobin was incensed and said so:

> Well, I mean, I think that's a real unfair to Anita Hill. I mean, Anita Hill wasn't just someone making accusations. There were corroborating witnesses. There were facts and allegations that he could have responded to and Steve Kroft could have asked him.

Other Thomas critics announced that they'd take to the airwaves to set the record straight about him. *CBS* was not one of the networks that offered Hill or anyone else airtime for any rebuttal.

*****

The notion that Thomas is not just a Judas and traitor but unfit to be called a real Black man bothered the man that Thomas had replaced on the high court, Thurgood Marshall. The liberal, activist, blunt-spoken, civil rights icon Marshall was everything that civil rights groups considered to be the stuff that makes up a real Black man. In other words, everything Thomas wasn't. But in a two-hour meeting after his nomination, Marshall warned Thomas that he would be held to a far harsher standard of scrutiny on and away from the bench than a white conservative in the same spot.

That insightful piece of advice from Marshall to Thomas was even more glaring in the way that civil rights leaders continued to link Thomas to Antonin Scalia even after the death of the ultra-conservative SCOTUS judge in 2016. Thomas, it was thought, was organically welded to Scalia in their lock-step judicial votes and opinions. Civil rights groups routinely slammed Thomas as Scalia's lackey—and continued to do that even after Scalia's death.

That was another way to say that Black conservatives are the puppets and white Republicans are the string-pullers. There was some fact and some fiction in that allegation. Analysts examined Thomas's and Scalia's votes on a range of issues and found that though they voted in lockstep on most issues, on some they didn't. There was just enough divergence in their positions that the analysts called it a "myth" that Thomas was a puppet of Scalia or the other conservative Justices.

In any case, Thomas bitterly resented that character-ization about him. In a speech to the National Bar Association in July 1998, Thomas pushed back hard against the knock that he was anyone's puppet, saying "Long gone is the time when we opposed the notion that we all looked alike and talked alike. Somehow, we have come to exalt the new black stereotype above all and to demand conformity to that norm... [However], I assert my right to think for myself, to refuse to have my ideas assigned to me as though I was an intellectual slave because I'm black."

*****

That has been Thomas's virtual mantra in defining his regal defiance of being racially pigeon-holed as inherently liberal and pro-civil rights because he's Black. That defiance of racial conventions has and continues to define Thomas through every waking moment of his tenure on the SCOTUS and in public life. This was something he would always take great pains to take pride in, no matter the cost of the legal and judicial damage he was accused by many of wreaking.

The instant the SCOTUS scrapped the use of affirmative action racial considerations in college admissions in June 2023, NAACP President Derrick Johnson got in the ultimate dig at Thomas: "The worst thing about affirmative action is that it created a Clarence Thomas, who benefited from the program and now is in a position where he's going to deny many young African American talented individuals an opportunity."

Johnson's dig at Thomas was not an unfair, below-the-belt hit. For decades before the court finally ruled on affirmative action, Thomas relentlessly led the charge against it. Typical of Thomas's obsessive loathing of affirmative action was an affirmative action case several years earlier.

In June 2016, the U.S. Supreme Court was poised to hand down another landmark decision on an affirmative action case. The case was the lawsuit brought by white student, Abigail Noel Fisher, against the University of Texas at Austin in which she claimed that race was the primary reason she was rejected for admission.

At the time, many legal experts and court watchers bet that the court would once and for all scrap the last vestiges of race as a factor in school admissions and by extension in employment. There was no bet, though, on how one Justice would vote. The Justice was, of course, Thomas.

His certain vote to uphold Fisher's case and dump race into the dustbin of legal and social history was so sure that it could almost have been mailed in. Thomas loudly told the world what he thought of affirmative action in his memoir, *My Grandfather's Son: A Memoir.* Here are his words:

> Affirmative action (though it wasn't yet called that) had become a fact of life at American colleges and universities, and before long I realized that those blacks who benefited from it were being judged by a double standard.
>
> The problem with my "adverse impact" analysis, of course, was that it was of no help to those black students who had already finished law school and now found themselves unable to pass the bar exam.
>
> The problems faced by blacks in America would take quite some time to solve, and the responsibility for solving them would fall largely on black people themselves.
>
> Most of the middle-class blacks with whom I discussed these policies argued that all blacks were equally disadvantaged by virtue of their race alone. I thought that was nonsense.

When Thomas cast his inevitable vote to expunge affirmative action, the one question that was asked of him then, as Johnson later chided him in 2023, was how and why someone who was at times a beneficiary of affirmative action could be the biggest hypocrite in opposing it.

First, there was the reminder of how much he had benefited. Despite his mediocre political credentials and undistinguished academic record, Thomas rose from junior Senate aide to Supreme Court Justice in less than a decade.

Here's the parade of plum positions that he got: Assistant Secretary of Education for Civil Rights, Chairman of the Equal Employment Opportunity Commission (EEOC), an appointment to the federal judiciary, and of course, Supreme Court Justice. His quick rise up the political and legal ladder was preceded by his race-based admission to Yale Law School. That drew the special ire of Thomas's critics particularly since neither he nor Yale officials denied it. The affirmative action program that got Thomas into Yale was a point of pride with school officials. It was the subject of an article in the *New York Times* in 1991, at the time of Thomas's confirmation debacle. Thomas again confirmed the veracity of it.

He noted that he was admitted, "under an explicit affirmative action plan with the goal of having blacks and other minority members make up about 10 percent of the entering class." Professor Abraham S. Goldstein, dean of the law school, from 1970 to 1975, was quoted by the *Times* as saying: "We did adopt an affirmative action program and it was pretty clearly stated."

A 1994 Yale Alumni Magazine article further confirmed it: "Like most American universities, Yale in the 1960s and '70s embarked on an aggressive policy of affirmative action in admitting and hiring minorities and women." It concluded: "Thomas has strongly supported the notion that his admission was under an affirmative action plan."

In his memoir, Thomas protested that he never actively sought these positions and pretended that he didn't want them because of his deep fear that he would be permanently tarred as an affirmative action hire. But no one twisted Thomas's arm or put a knife to his throat and demanded that he accept any of these positions, including admission to Yale Law School.

He had a mouth, and he could have opened it and said "no" every time he was offered a professional leg up. He didn't. If Thomas had just taken the plums served up to him, and quietly melted into the woodwork with his titles, it would have been harmless enough. But he had a bigger agenda in mind, and that was to be an aggressive and relentless foe of the very affirmative action measures that he milked.

*****

The Supreme Court post gave Thomas the ideal power position to advance his agenda and do real damage. The pounding he took during his high court confirmation fight in 1991 from civil rights, civil liberties, and women's groups, and the narrow Senate vote to confirm him stung him deeply.

Thomas didn't forget or forgive. When asked how long he'd stay on the court, he reportedly said that he'd stay there for the next forty-three years of his life. He was forty-three at the time. By the time of the June 2023 SCOTUS decision on affirmative action, Thomas had become one of the longest-serving Justices on the court.

In a more revealing aside, he supposedly quipped to friends that it would take him that long to get even. Whether this was hyperbole or an apocryphal tale, it didn't take him forty-three years to wreak his revenge. He made no effort to mask his mission on the court, and that was to expunge race from law and public policy decisions.

However, this was not simply one man's bitterness over his alleged mistreatment by liberals and civil rights leaders. In well-prepped and orchestrated talks to ultra-conservative groups, Thomas pretty much made it clear that his quest was to make sure law and public policy in America mirrored his own take on race.

The capper was his swipe at President Obama in an April 2013 talk at Duquesne Law School. He implied that Obama was an affirmative action President and that the "elites" embraced him because he was Black. Presumably, Thomas meant liberal Democrats and maybe racially guilt-stricken whites.

Thomas's conservative, unorthodox views and legal opinions on the death penalty, age and gender bias, the First Amendment, prisoner rights, and affirmative action cases were well known by the time he hit the court in 1991. It could hardly be said that Thomas latched on to judicial conservatism solely to curry favor with white conservatives and snatch a seat on the Supreme Court.

Yet the belief that he did guarantee that he would be the man that civil rights groups and Democrats would perennially castigate as the Black who got away. The huge boost he got up the education and career ladder because of affirmative action had the opposite effect. His impassioned and obsessive assault on it proved that.

4

Obama Under Thomas's Fire

"Perhaps some are confused because they have stereotypes of how blacks should be and I respectfully decline, as I did in my youth, to sacrifice who I am for who they think I should be."

In December 2008, the SCOTUS gave short shrift to yet another lawsuit demanding disclosure about whether then President-elect Barack Obama was a U.S. citizen or not. Before that, in October 2008, a federal appeals court in New Jersey also tossed a similar lawsuit. In the case of the SCOTUS, it was left to then Justice David Souter to reject the lawsuit. He denied a stay to get Obama removed from the ballot in New Jersey.

That didn't end the matter. Thomas saw to that. He took the almost unprecedented step of reopening the issue by agreeing to put the matter to a conference vote. Thomas's ridiculous lone-wolf effort to arm-twist the Justices to examine the birth certificate issue made no sense to most legal experts. Obama was born in Hawaii. And by then he had produced more than enough evidence to back that up.

Thomas's legal meddling on the Obama birth certificate non-issue fit in perfectly with his intrinsic interpretation of the law and its practice, and his private vow to get back at his liberal tormentors. Obama was simply the latest would-be victim. He almost certainly stirred Thomas's ire in August 2008.

Obama was asked at a joint gathering with Republican presidential opponent John McCain at the Saddleback megachurch in Lake Forest, California which Justice he wouldn't have nominated to the Supreme Court. He didn't hesitate. He named Thomas. And he told why:

> I don't think that he was a strong enough jurist or legal thinker at the time, for that elevation, setting aside the fact that I profoundly disagree with his interpretations of a lot of the constitution.

*****

Even if Obama hadn't zinged Thomas publicly, he still would have been in his sights. He was the opposite of Thomas. He was a moderate Democrat, a former civil rights attorney, and a community organizer. He backed expanded government, affirmative action, abortion rights, a severely restricted use of the death penalty and, to the absolute horror of Thomas and hardline conservatives, he backed a broader interpretation of legal precepts.

Obama almost certainly would have joined the swollen chorus of civil rights and civil liberties groups that pounded Thomas during his 1991 confirmation fight for his anti-affirmative action, anti-abortion, and anti-prisoner rights views. The Senate confirmed him by the narrowest vote of any high court judge in recent confirmation history. There is little doubt that if Obama had been in the Senate then, he would have been one of the most vociferous opponents of Thomas's confirmation.

The rebuke stung deeply, and Thomas didn't forget or forgive. In an *American Enterprise Institute* lecture in 2001, he again voiced intense anger at his perceived ill-treatment by liberals. He said that he expected to be treated badly for challenging liberal opinion.

This, though, was not simply one man's bitterness over his alleged mistreatment by liberals and civil rights leaders. Nor was it a case of Thomas digging his heels in to push his retrograde view on legal matters. He wanted more judges to think and act like him on the bench. Obama had made it clear not only that he would not appoint another Thomas to the Supreme Court, but that the type of Justices he'd appoint would be the diametric opposite of him. At the time there was a good chance that he would have had that chance, maybe even two or possibly three chances, to appoint liberal, moderate justices to the SCOTUS.

Midway through Obama's two White House terms from 2008 to 2016, the court's liberals, Ruth Bader Ginsberg, John Paul Stevens, and Stephen Breyer, and the moderate to conservative Anthony Kennedy were in their seventies. Obama would likely have picked like-minded judicially philosophical judges to replace one or more of them. This would have decisively thwarted Thomas and the conservatives' well-planned and designed court counter-revolution.

A McCain win in the 2008 presidential election would have ensured that there would be even more Justices who would likely see eye to eye with Thomas on abortion, affirmative action, the death penalty, prisoner rights, and outgoing President George W. Bush's war on terrorism orders.

That didn't happen. McCain lost. But federal appeals courts in future years would still deal with the sensitive issues of abortion rights, minimum mandatory sentencing, DNA testing in capital cases, search and seizure laws, and racial profiling. Those cases would ultimately wind their way up to the Supreme Court. The rulings and dissents in these cases would permanently reshape America's legal landscape, for good and bad.

*****

Thomas's votes to overturn *Roe* in 2022 and affirmative action in college admissions in June 2023, as well as all other cases involving conservative flashpoint issues, were predictable. For a time, Obama's White House wins guaranteed that there wouldn't be other Justices whose votes were just as predictable and in agreement with his. However, that did not deter Thomas in the least once Obama was out of office, and the SCOTUS had a firm conservative majority that Thomas wanted, and Obama had tried to thwart. Obama was mindful of the huge threat Thomas and a hard-nosed rightist SCOTUS posed to his liberal judicial philosophy.

Immediately after the SCOTUS's June 2023 decision to scrap affirmative action in college admissions, with Thomas playing a lead role in that, Obama was the paragon of tact and circumspection regarding Thomas. He did not single him out in his criticism of the court's decision. He simply said that while affirmative action was "never a complete answer," the policy gave students "who had been systematically excluded from most of America's key institutions" a chance to "show we more than deserved a seat at the table. In the wake of the Supreme Court's recent decision, it's time to redouble our efforts."

Thomas's shot-in-the-dark effort to make an issue of Obama's birth certificate was simply another foray in Thomas's ongoing battle to totally refashion law and public policy in America in his conservative mold. Obama was just another foil for him in that.

5

Thomas's Continuing Payback

"It really bugs me that someone will tell me, after I spent twenty years being educated, how I'm supposed to think."

Following the heavy fallout from the SCOTUS's final rejection of the use of race criteria as a factor in college admissions in June 2023, two words were increasingly being said, both quietly and openly, about the Supreme Court. The words were, "Thomas's court."

This was not hyperbole. At the time of the decision, Thomas was the current longest-sitting judge on the court. His "originalist," strict constructionist views—that is the view that the Constitution and other laws should be understood according to the conventional meaning of the text when ratified or enacted by the Founding Fathers—were embraced and embedded in his dissents and opinions. They were now, to one degree or another, embedded in the opinions and rulings of the majority of the court's Justices.

Thomas's new-found unabashed power and influence was at work. And he knew it. He had emerged forcefully from the shadows and opaqueness that he had calculatingly shrouded himself in for decades on the court. His long-winded written rationale for voting to strike down affirmative action in college admissions was a big, aggressive, forceful statement that he had finally arrived as a, if not the, major power broker on the court.

*****

This was the fulfillment of Thomas's long ambition, as well as a validation of his long game to upstage his legion of dogged, unforgiving detractors. And at the same time he was bending the court to his will and philosophy.

Thomas's power and confidence were so immense that court Justices were silent, turned a blind eye, or uttered the most unconvincing of promises to exercise better ethics scrutiny over Thomas's outrageous flaunting of the requirement to disclose gifts and perks received from cheerleading donors and friends. While some Democrats screamed for his head (namely impeachment), Thomas was smugly comfortable in the knowledge that the calls would be just that—calls. They almost certainly would ultimately come to nothing.

Thomas's many defenders turned the table on the Democrat's threatened calls for ethics probes of him. They simply viewed this as further proof of his leap to the forefront as a court power broker. Said one, "It's a kind of sore loserism taken to a whole new level."

The now suddenly openly impactful Thomas showed another side to reinforce his stature as the court conservatives' point man. He talked. For years, Thomas was the butt of jokes about his clam-like refusal to utter a single word, let alone ask a question or make a quip during oral arguments before the judges in cases.

Thomas on occasion was asked why he never uttered a word for more than a decade on the bench. He has offered a variety of reasons for his silence from the bench.

Here was one answer he gave, "We have a lifetime to go back in chambers and to argue with each other. The lawyers only have about thirty minutes to present their side of the case. They should argue. That's part of the process." He added that he didn't like to "badger people."

That changed in 2020 in a trademark protection case. Thomas now became the aggressive questioner of attorneys.

"A couple of questions," Thomas began, "Could Booking acquire an 800 number that's a vanity number—1-800-BOOKING, for example—that is similar to 1-800-PLUMBING, which is a registered mark?" He continued, "Well, that could be true. I'd like you to compare this to *Goodyear*."

"In *Goodyear*, you had a generic term, but you also had added a term such as company or Inc. which any company could use. Now, with Booking, there could only be one domain address dot com. So this would seem to be more analogous to the 1-800 numbers which are also individualized."

Thomas's question garnered lots of stunned and incredulous press attention. Yet, it left no doubt that his days of silence, seeming passivity, and inertia were over.

*****

The decisive turning point in Thomas's fortunes as a court conservative leader came in 2022. The defining moment was the case *New York State Rifle & Pistol Association v. Bruen*. This permitted the right to carry firearms for self-defense outside of the home. The shield again was the Second Amendment.

This case was tailor-made for Thomas. He could apply his hard-wired "originalist" view of the Constitution to the issue. In this case, he wrote the majority opinion that upheld almost unlimited gun owner rights, citing the Second Amendment. The decision virtually directed lower courts to apply the same strict construction ruling in deciding similar cases. His message: the Second Amendment should be understood the same way it would have been interpreted at the time of its adoption.

Thomas watchers were quick to note how Thomas, after this decision and the prime role he played in it, had now moved front and center to change the judicial game on the SCOTUS. "The story isn't so much that Thomas has changed, but that the court has changed around him," observed Columbia Law School professor, Olatunde Johnson. She added that the Thomas court is "unequivocally a more conservative court than when he joined. That not only makes him no longer isolated on the court but could even make Thomas feel bolder in his jurisprudence."

Not "could" but almost certainly "would" embolden him. It didn't take long to see that. In the court's decision to scrap *Roe* and abortion in June 2022, Thomas didn't just simply cast the predictable affirmative vote. He went further and virtually demanded that the court take action to scrap the court's favorable decisions on "fundamental rights" such as the use of contraceptives, same-sex marriage, and even interracial marriage.

At that point, Thomas was five years away from setting the record as being the longest-serving judge in court history. If he set that record, given the increasingly tight lock of the conservative majority, Thomas had a better than even chance of seeing much of his dream of torpedoing those rights become a dreaded, nightmare reality. The conservative majority's ruling to eliminate affirmative action in college admissions was a telling example of Thomas's putting his indelible mark on the court, said one Thomas watcher.

Thomas's emergence as the new guiding light on the court in 2023 came full circle back to his being a man of his word. Since that fateful day in 1991, when by the narrowest of margins, a deeply divided and even more deeply reluctant Senate confirmed him to the Supreme Court, Thomas vowed payback against those who ridiculed, reviled, and hounded him during the confirmation fight. He would never forget that humiliation.

He proved that first in yet another of his patented one-man dissents against the court's February 2013 majority ruling to not scrap a key section of the Voting Rights Act. Thomas went against his fellow hardline, strict constructionist, Justice Scalia in his dissent. He argued that he'd dump the Act since, as he put it, "The extensive pattern of discrimination that led the Court to previously uphold Section 5 ...no longer exists."

It did, and the other eight Justices, Scalia included, obviously were bothered enough by the briefs from civil rights groups that implored the court to uphold the Act. They fully documented that more than a few districts in the South and the West used rigged or malfunctioning voting machines, selective photo IDs, contrived language requirements, alleged ballot shortages, the absence of polling places and registrars, the selective use of felon laws, and intimidation tactics to chase as many Blacks, Latinos, and American Indians from the polls as possible. The Justice Department had filed dozens of voting irregularity and discrimination complaints during the Obama administration years from 2008 to 2016.

A decade later in June 2023, Thomas was back at it again. He was furious that the justices, by a 5 to 4 decision, struck down Alabama's blatant move to racially gerrymander districts to dilute Black voting strength in violation of the 1965 Voting Rights Act. Thomas was in top belligerent form in penning an angry, nearly fifty-page dissent that ripped anything he saw as promoting a racial preference. He called the court's VRA decision "nothing more than a racial entitlement to roughly proportional control of elective offices—limited only by feasibility—wherever different racial groups consistently prefer different candidates."

He wasn't finished. He blustered that the Voting Rights Act doesn't require Alabama to "intentionally redraw its longstanding congressional districts so that black voters can control a number of seats roughly proportional to the black share of the State's population."

*****

Thomas's contrarian votes on race-based court cases of course made no sense to most legal experts. But his decisions made sense because they had less to do with his warped interpretation of law and its practice than with his publicly expressed racial views, and his private vow to get revenge.

In his memoir, *My Grandfather's Son*, he branded those who reviled him as the "liberal mob." He returned to his constant theme that they had one goal and only one goal, and that was to "keep the black man in his place." The Black man of course was Thomas.

The other theme that coursed through Thomas's clinical need for payback was his obsessive view of himself as the eternal outcast. In that American Enterprise Institute lecture in 2001, the title "Be Not Afraid" was in part a characterization of how he felt that he was constantly hectored by civil rights groups for his conservatism. In greater part, it was meant to be a bold, defiant, and aggressive warning that he would not change one iota his position on the issues and would continue to punch away on the court to further his agenda.

Thomas's views and legal opinions on the death penalty, age and gender bias, the First Amendment, prisoner rights, and affirmative action cases were at the time of his taking a seat on the Supreme Court in 1991 still a distinct minority opinion of most of the other Justices. This often made Thomas the solitary figure in his dissents from court majority opinions on these judicially and politically sensitive issues.

There were some cases in which Thomas cast the only dissenting vote. However, he was undeterred. He believed what he said and wrote even when others didn't and couldn't. But even if he didn't, he still would have said and written the unbending case dissents and opinions he did.

By 2023, Thomas had established a firm pattern of being a lone dissenter in court cases that had even the remotest tie to a conservative-favored issue. Former President Donald Trump's ferocious effort to get the SCOTUS to uphold his right to refuse to turn over documents to a House Select investigating committee was a prime example.

Thomas's five conservative companion Justices quickly shot down Trump's request. Not Thomas. Here's exactly what the SCOTUS published about its decision: "The application for stay of mandate and injunction pending review presented to THE CHIEF JUSTICE and by him referred to the Court is denied." It later states "JUSTICE THOMAS would grant the application."

Thomas gave no reason for his one-man vote that swam against the court tide, including that of the other court conservatives. In truth, his seemingly meaningless dissent was no surprise. He was simply fulfilling his vow of payback.

6

Anita Hill's Long Shadow

"And I thank God I believe in God, or I would probably be enormously angry right now."

"I still believe in Anita Hill." This chant from a few students came at the end of Thomas's lecture on faith and his judicial and political views at Notre Dame University in September 2021. Thomas appeared unruffled by the outburst. The students were roundly booed and then quickly dragooned out of the auditorium by security to loud applause. It was a small, seemingly pinprick demonstration.

However, the fact that it happened at all, three decades after Anita Hill nearly upended his confirmation to the SCOTUS in 1991 with her riveting accusation against him of sexual harassment and misconduct, was telling. To many, Thomas would be forever linked to Hill and the issue of sexual harassment.

In the decades since the Thomas-Hill imbroglio, a parade of top-name celebrities, media luminaries, athletes, and especially politicians, both Republicans and Democrats, were slapped with charges of sexual misconduct. One especially notable noted political official, hit with the charge of sexual malfeasance, conjured up again the memory of Thomas and Hill. That was New York Representative Anthony Weiner. He ultimately resigned in disgrace in June 2011.

*****

Thomas did not comment on Weiner's downfall. But he almost certainly breathed a big sigh of relief. There was much talk the year before Weiner resigned that he would be the point man on the House Judiciary Committee if it decided to go after Thomas for his long trail of financial manipulations, abuse, and duplicity.

Weiner gave some hope that he'd be the go-to guy against Thomas because he had been hammering him and his wife, Virginia, publicly on his dealings and demanding that he recuse himself from any Supreme Court deliberations and ruling on the constitutionality of the then-contentious Affordable Care Act that conservatives loathed.

Weiner pulled no punches in a March 2011 *Fox News* interview. He demanded Thomas recuse himself from the court's pending decision regarding the legality of the Act because of his and his wife's dubious conflicting interests with right-wing groups fighting the Act. Weiner sharply noted, "What it comes down to is a pretty clear federal law that requires judges and justices to recuse themselves whenever there is ... an appearance of any bias in the case." The law, he said, "has certain categories where you must recuse yourself, and one of them is if you or your household, your spouse has any financial interest in the outcome. And we found out recently that Ginni Thomas, the spouse of Justice Thomas, has received more than $700,000 from organizations whose existence is based on making sure the health care law is ruled unconstitutional." Weiner added that "It got worse over the weekend because Justice Thomas said he agreed with his wife."

Legal scholars were divided on this. Some sided with Thomas. Others sided with Weiner and said there was an obligation for him to step aside in the case. It was a moot point. Thomas had no intention of sitting that one out. The issue was too close to his stern view that the Act had no Constitutional justification.

Weiner certainly had a lot of ammunition to make Thomas's alleged misdoings a prima facie legal and political embarrassment for the GOP. This stemmed from Thomas's wife Virginia's mini-king's ransom earnings she received from assorted right-wing foundations and think tanks. The Heritage Foundation was a prominent funder of her, as well as the ultraconservative Koch brothers, the Coors family, and Richard Mellon Scaife, all of whom had a major interest in any number of Supreme Court rulings.

Thomas did disclose his wife's earnings. He did not disclose speaking fees and perks he got from a bevy of the same conservative groups that his wife worked for and had close political ties to. And then he refused to acknowledge her involvement with Liberty Central. This is the outfit that gained notoriety for hectoring then-President Obama on any and every one of his policy issues, especially his Affordable Care Act. Thomas's wife famously bragged at the time that she aimed to make the organization "bigger than the tea party." She took dead aim at Obama's agenda.

*****

This was almost secondary to the resurrection of Hill as Thomas's foil. There was the strong hint that Thomas perjured himself in his testimony to the Senate Judiciary Committee during his court confirmation hearings in 1991 and that he compounded that by lying under oath to Congress during the hearings.

Thomas was asked directly by then Utah senator Orrin Hatch during his confirmation hearings about Anita Hill's allegations of sexual harassment and misconduct and whether he used sexually suggestive language. Thomas answered: "I deny each and every single allegation against me today that suggested in any way that I had conversations of a sexual nature or about pornographic material with Anita Hill, that I ever attempted to date her, that I ever had any personal sexual interest in her, or that I in any way ever harassed her."

Thomas was emphatic: "If I used that kind of grotesque language with one person, it would seem to me that there would be traces of it throughout the employees who worked closely with me, or the other individuals who heard bits and pieces of it or various levels of it." This was stated under oath to the Senate Judiciary Committee. Thomas's sworn testimony was clearly contradicted even then in public statements by witnesses. These witnesses were not called to testify.

Two decades later, in October 2010, Thomas's apparently perjured testimony to Congress was back on the legal table when another Thomas intimate confirmed that he engaged in sexual harassment, was addicted to pornography and talked incessantly and graphically about it, and that the women were truthful.

Ironically, what triggered the reinterest in Thomas-Hill was nothing Thomas said or did in the intervening years, but Thomas's wife. She demanded in a phone message to Hill that she "consider something. I would love you to consider an apology sometime and some full explanation of why you did what you did with my husband." That wasn't going to happen. But it made the news and the public cast an eye back on Thomas and sexual misconduct again.

It's also clearly established that a public official—whether the president, presidential appointees, or judges—can be punished for giving false information (and that's any false information, of any nature) to the House or Senate. Close scrutiny by House Democrats of Thomas's possible wrongdoing was taken off the Congressional table when the Republicans took back control of the House in November 2010. And Thomas's financial misdoings and dubious confirmation hearing testimony quickly fell from the news.

*****

With the 2012 elections then nearing and the possibility that the Democrats could either win back control of the House or substantially boost their numbers there, Thomas's financial double-dealing and shadowy political ties could easily have been back on the political table.

Weiner showed intense interest in Thomas's doings, and his public hectoring of Thomas during the health care debate about his financial dealings sent a mild signal that Thomas at some point could be fair game for a probe. That would have done much to further expose the financial, legal, and moral misdeeds by conservatives that the GOP routinely sweeps under the rug.

Thomas and the GOP ultimately didn't have to worry about that. Thomas's potential tormentor was out of the House and Democrats were content to put the Weiner and the Thomas matter behind them. But the shouts from student demonstrators at Notre Dame in 2021, a decade after Weiner's congressional departure, were another testament to the enduring shadow that Hill would continue to cast over Thomas.

7

Trump's Favorite Judge

"My job is to write opinions. I decide cases and write opinions. It is not to respond to idiocy and critics who make statements that are unfounded. That doesn't mean that people shouldn't have constructive criticisms, but it should be constructive."

In January 2021, former President Trump badly needed an ace card on the Supreme Court. Nearly every court and nearly every judge had flatly turned down his appeal to stop the certification of the 2020 presidential election which Biden had won, and Trump loudly refused to accept. He thought he might have one last legal card to play in the one Justice whom he believed would likely be the most sympathetic to his appeal. That Justice was Thomas.

Trump had filed his last-ditch effort with the SCOTUS to stop the certification of Biden as president and Thomas would be one of the Justices who would rule on his appeal. Trump's attorney Kenneth Chesebro spelled out Trump's hope and strategy in courting Thomas in a December 31, 2021, email: "We want to frame things so that Thomas could be the one to issue some sort of stay or other circuit justice opinion saying Georgia is in legitimate doubt." He was clear that Thomas would be "our only chance to get a favorable judicial opinion by January 6, which might hold up the Georgia count in Congress."

Trump courted Thomas for three reasons. The first was pragmatic. Thomas was assigned by the SCOTUS to handle any emergency matters out of Georgia for the Supreme Court. He would have the say-so over whether the court should consider a case or an appeal from there. If Thomas agreed to consider the Trump anti-Biden certification appeal, that could be the spark that Trump needed to get GOP-controlled legislatures and GOP congressional representatives to jump back on Trump's anti-Biden certification bandwagon.

Thomas was more than just a Hail Mary ploy by Trump. He had earlier shown much sympathy for Trump's flailing effort to boost his bogus presidential win claim. He said that if the Supreme Court had accepted Trump's earlier appeal to challenge the vote count in four states, he would have accepted jurisdiction over the case. The court turned the appeal down.

The second reason Trump put much hope in a Thomas bail-out was Thomas's wife Virginia. She had made clear that she totally bought into Trump's claim that the election was stolen from him. She went further and actively lobbied legislators in two pivotal states, Arizona and Wisconsin, to toss out the vote for Biden. When the revelation of her behind-the-scenes wheeling and dealing for Trump was publicly exposed, she fervently denied that her impassioned pro-Trump advocacy had influenced her husband in any way.

It required a great deal of credulity to believe that. Trump and his legal team certainly knew better. There was near-smoking gun proof of that in a couple of the cases that did come before the SCOTUS, in which the GOP pushed its overblown, silly charge of election fraud.

Thomas had a lot to say about the issue in those cases. In one notable comment, he made clear what he thought: "An election system lacks clear rules when, as here, different officials dispute who has authority to set or change those rules. This kind of dispute brews confusion because voters may not know which rules to follow. Even worse … competing candidates might each declare victory under different sets of rules." This was virtually an open endorsement of the GOP charge of election fraud and an open license for Trump to continue to hector the courts, saying that he was a victim of that alleged fraud.

*****

This tied directly in with the third reason Trump viewed Thomas as his best chance to get some legal traction on his fraudulent claim of election theft. He had repeatedly said in years past that he ranked Thomas, along with Scalia, as his kind of judge. During the presidential campaign in 2016, Trump's cheerleading of the two Justices upped the ante on arguably the single biggest campaign issue that backers of both Trump and his Democratic rival Hillary Clinton were the most anxious about. That was: who got to appoint someone to the Supreme Court during the next four to eight years of the winner's term or terms?

At the time, the prospect was that there could be anywhere from two to four vacancies in that period. Trump upped the ante in three ways. The first was when he again tossed out Scalia's name during his acceptance speech at the Republican National Convention in August 2016. This was not simply a doubling down on his praise of Scalia as the Justice who, along with Thomas, was at the top of his Supreme Court heroes list. It sent the strongest signal that his picks would not just be garden variety strict constructionists, but activists and influencers on the bench. They would be Justices who wouldn't base their rulings solely on the standard conservative playbook but would cajole, hector, and badger other Justices to toe the conservative line in their rulings—and who would have the gall when it suited their purpose, to not even try and hide it.

Thomas was the perfect example of this kind of Justice. He was in perfect harmony with Scalia who didn't even try to make a constitutional cover for his push to give Florida to Bush in the 2000 election controversy. As he famously and shamelessly said, "The only issue was whether we should put an end to it, after three weeks of looking like a fool in the eyes of the world." Thomas heartily agreed with that pro-Bush sentiment.

Nowhere was Scalia's impact on Thomas on more stunning display than for the two decades that he served as the court schoolmaster for him. During that time, Scalia ensured that the other Justices looked hard over their shoulders at him when they huddled to craft an opinion in a case, Thomas with few rare exceptions included.

It was no accident that after Scalia's death in 2016, it looked and even sounded at times like an almost moderate court in some of its rulings: on abortion rights, affirmative action, voting rights, and the feds paying for contraceptives at religious hospitals. The outcomes would have almost certainly been different if Scalia had been there. In all of these affirmative liberal ruling decisions, Thomas dissented.

*****

Thomas recognized at the time the influence Scalia had on the court, and the effect on him: "I have warm relationships with everybody on the court and especially with my colleagues, but Justice Scalia was special in that he had been at the court about five years when I got there when I was forty-three years old and had only been a judge about a year and a half, so this was all new to me."

During the 2016 presidential campaign, then GOP Vice Presidential contender Mike Pence made the Trump-Scalia-Thomas axis official when he vowed to a campaign crowd in Michigan that Trump's Supreme Court picks would hit the bench with the practically sworn duty to slam down the curtain on Roe v. Wade. This was tantamount to promising to say to heck with law, prior rulings, or deliberations; the Justice would just knock out abortion rights, period.

Pence didn't stop there. He repeatedly tossed out the mantra that Trump would select strict constructionists for his appointments, and not just for a Thomas-Scalia-type judicial hit on abortion rights. This was a prime advertisement for unapologetic conservative judicial activism in the cookie-cutter mold of a Thomas.

Trump didn't publicly drop Scalia and Thomas's names solely because he considered them the Justices with the right stuff. They were Justices whom he knew, above all others, were considered demigods among party ultra-conservatives, pro-lifers, and evangelicals. By invoking their names, he burnished his credentials among them.

Many had voiced big doubts about Trump's less-than-stout conservative pronouncements about abortion, Planned Parenthood, religious values, and law and public policy decisions as translated by the courts. That made it even more imperative for Trump to send the signal that he would move mountains to find and nominate Thomas-type activist judges to the Supreme Court.

*****

In decades past, many Democratic and Republican-appointed Justices scrapped party loyalties and based their legal decisions solely on the merit of the law, constitutional principles, and the public good. Thomas was a judicial horse of a different color. The tip-off that judges like him would vote for their ideology rather than the law came from George W. Bush. On the presidential campaign trail in 2000, Bush was asked, if elected, what kind of judge he'd look for and nominate. He didn't hesitate. He pledged to appoint "strict constructionists" to the court and specifically named Thomas, Scalia, and William Rehnquist as the Justices who perfectly fit that description. By then the three had already carved out a hardline niche as three of the most reflexive, knee-jerk, reactionary jurists to grace the court in decades. Their votes to torpedo, water down, eviscerate, or erode rights on all issues from abortion to civil rights were always pro forma.

A Supreme Court Justice can sit on the court for years, even decades, and watch as legions of Republicans and Democrats come and go in Congress and the White House. Thomas certainly did. All the while, a SCOTUS Justice can shape and remake law and public policy for decades to come with their votes, rulings, and opinions. Trump may not have known much else about judicial workings, but he knew that a few more Thomases on the bench would ensure that the Supreme Court did just that, and in his way.

Trump failed in his last-ditch, desperate Hail Mary effort to rope Thomas into aiding and abetting his bizarre plot to overturn the 2020 presidential election results. But it certainly wasn't due to any unwillingness on Thomas's part to help him do just that.

8

Impeach Thomas?

"I began to suspect that Daddy had been right all along: The only hope I had of changing the world was to change myself first. I thought of the many times that he and I had delivered fresh-picked farm produce to one of our elderly relatives. On such occasions he never failed to remind me that if we hadn't worked so hard to grow it, we wouldn't be able to give it to those who needed help."

"This degree of corruption is shocking—almost cartoonish," New York Democratic congressional representative Alexandria Ocasio-Cortez, wrote on Twitter, "Thomas must be impeached." Ocasio-Cortez could not have been blunter in her April 5, 2023, tweet about what Thomas's fate should be. She was hardly a lone voice in demanding Thomas's ouster. Sponsors of an online MoveOn.org petition announced in July 2023 that they had more than one million signers on their petition titled "Impeach Justice Clarence Thomas." "He must resign—or Congress must immediately investigate and impeach," the petition boldly stated.

Ocasio-Cortez and the million or more signers of the petition were hardly the first to call for Thomas's removal. In fact, Thomas was no stranger to calls for his resignation or impeachment. There were several over the years he's been on the Supreme Court. One of these attempts merits particular note. A decade earlier, in 2011, many were convinced that the grounds for impeachment proceedings against him were virtually iron-clad. The evidence seemed compelling that Thomas had perjured himself in his testimony to the Senate Judiciary Committee during his court confirmation hearings in 1991. The evidence seemed equally compelling that this constituted lying under oath to Congress.

The impeachment case against Thomas was not based on personal or political disagreement over his views, decisions, opinions, and rulings on the bench, his penchant for pornographic material, or for sexual harassment. It was based on clear legal and constitutional grounds, precedents, and Congressional mandates. Article III, Section 1 of the U.S. Constitution explicitly states that a Supreme Court Justice who "lacks good behavior" can be impeached. This is not an ambiguous, subjective term. It has been interpreted by the courts to equate to the same level of seriousness as the "high crimes and misdemeanors" clause that unequivocally mandates that the House of Representatives initiate impeachment proceedings against any public official or federal judge in violation of that provision.

This Constitutional precept was the first legal ground for impeachment proceedings against Thomas. The second was Title 18 of the U.S. Code. It states that any official of the executive, legislative, or judicial branch of the government of the United States who knowingly and willfully falsifies, conceals, or covers up by any trick, scheme, or device a material fact; makes any materially false, fictitious, or fraudulent statement or representation; or makes or uses any false writing or document knowing the same to contain any materially false, fictitious, or fraudulent statement or entry can be impeached.

In other words, lying to Congress was not only an impeachable offense. It's also illegal. It's also clearly established that a public official—whether the president, presidential appointees, or judges—can be punished for giving false information and that's any false information of any nature to the House or Senate.

*****

The Nixon impeachment debates following the Watergate revelations in 1974 and the Clinton impeachment hearings in 1998 were ample proof that the constitutional phrase of "good behavior" embraces not only indictable crimes but "conduct ... grossly incompatible with the office held and subversive of that office and of our constitutional system of government."

Many, as noted, tried hard to make the case that Thomas had lied about his relationship and actions toward Hill during his confirmation hearing. Thomas was under sworn oath.

Thomas's sworn testimony was clearly contradicted even then in public statements by witnesses. The witnesses were not called to testify. Only one witness who contradicted Thomas's sworn testimony, Angela Wright, did testify. She worked with Thomas at the Equal Employment Opportunity Commission and was emphatic that Thomas sexually harassed her and used explicit and graphic sexual language.

Her story was corroborated by a former EEOC speechwriter who told investigators about Thomas's penchant for improper sexual talk. Letters to the committee from other women who worked with Thomas confirmed that he was a serial sexual harasser and had a penchant for sexually perverse talk. The Senate panel had other sources to corroborate the Hill-Wright charges that Thomas engaged in sexual harassment and obsessive interest in sexual smut. These sources were ignored, too.

Two decades later, Thomas's apparently perjured testimony to Congress was now squarely back on the legal table. Lillian McEwen put it there. Her legal credentials were impressive. She was a former assistant U.S. attorney and Senate Judiciary Committee counsel. She had also dated Thomas. In interviews, she again confirmed that Hill and the other women's allegations that Thomas engaged in sexual harassment, was addicted to pornography and talked incessantly and graphically about it and about women were truthful.

*****

Thomas's alleged warped sexual predilections and perversions were not the issue, as personally reprehensible as some may find them. The issue was his apparently perjured testimony to a congressional body about his words and conduct. There is no statute of limitations on bringing impeachment proceedings against officials who lie to Congress. The U.S. Code and the Constitution spell out that when there's evidence a Supreme Court justice may have lied under oath, the House must bring articles of impeachment to determine guilt or innocence.

But could that happen to Thomas? "Another day, another conflict of interest for Justice Thomas revealed. Add this to the laundry list of impeachable offenses he has committed. He has no business being on the Supreme Court, and no shame," tweeted Democratic Representative Jan Schakowsky in April 2023.

Again, legal scholars were divided on impeaching him, with the majority of those who weighed in on it saying that the odds are slim to none. Under Article I of the Constitution, Congress has the power to impeach a judge. It can be done by a simple majority. But as with an impeachment action against a President, there must be a senate trial with two-thirds of the Senators voting to convict.

No SCOTUS Justice has been impeached since 1804. That dubious distinction goes to Samuel Chase. He was impeached by the House for extreme political partisanship in his court decisions. Chase didn't leave the bench. He was acquitted in the Senate. His crime per the impeachment charge, ironically, is eerily similar to the charge repeatedly leveled against Thomas by critics: that he is dogmatically rightist and politically partisan.

"Unfortunately for the country, there is very little that can be done about this since Supreme Court justices are not held to an ethical code of conduct and because the chances of Thomas being impeached are slim to none," said Paul Collins, a legal studies and political science professor at the University of Massachusetts Amherst. "So, while there may be an investigation in Congress, I do not believe any serious action will be taken against Thomas, which will add to the impression that the justices are above the law."

That of course did not happen in 2011. However, in the decade following this major call for Thomas's impeachment, Thomas continued to skirt the law and ethics requirements in his dubious financial dealings with rich, powerful, ultra-conservative donors. He thumbed his nose at those who demanded he comply with the rules on disclosure. His hard-nosed, contrarian opinions conformed to the letter with the political stance of his ultra-conservative financial benefactors.

Thomas had not changed his ways or mode of operation one bit in his decades on and off the court. This ensured that the word "impeachment" would always hover in the air when Thomas's name was mentioned. The likelihood as always, though, was that it would end there with no action against him.

Ocasio-Cortez, who demanded his impeachment, probably had the last word on the futility of pursuing a Thomas impeachment. In an April 2023 interview on CNN's State of the Union, she essentially threw in the towel on the issue, "I admit it is very difficult to see a path in a Republican Party that refuses to hold itself accountable and, in fact, breaches the law itself. For all of their talk of a crime wave and Democrats, and Republicans talking about crime waves across the country, the crime wave is within the Republican Party."

9

Clarence Thomas on Clarence Thomas

"I certainly have some very strong libertarian leanings, yes."

For much of the time Thomas that has been on the SCO-TUS, he earned his much-deserved reputation as the Justice who came closest to being Sphinx-like when people were trying to figure out what he actually would say about the many controversial cases that came before the court. Thomas stirred this wonderment because during oral arguments by attorneys before the court he rarely uttered a word of questioning, let alone offered an opinion.

Thomas may have been a classic Silent Sam type during those years, but he was anything but silent when it came to voicing his opinions on a range of politically charged pinprick issues. He voiced his opinions in the venues that he chose and the times he chose. Those venues were almost exclusively carefully chosen appearances before cozy, adoring conservative groups. At other times, he expressed himself in his often-dissenting opinions. Whichever way, he always carefully picked his spots.

*****

Here's a sampling of some of Thomas's more quotable pointed notions on flashpoint law and public policy issues. The first is his view of how the Constitution's precepts should be applied to issues. One of the issues that he drew heavy fire on from civil rights groups was prisoner rights. In a case in 1992, he infuriated every civil rights and prisoner rights group by opposing the majority decision to uphold the suit by a prisoner who had been beaten to a pulp by prison guards in Louisiana while in shackles. Thomas saw no merit in the prisoner's Eighth Amendment claim that the beating was a blatant case of cruel and unusual punishment.

> "In my view, a use of force that causes only insignificant harm to a prisoner may be immoral, it may be tortious, it may be criminal, and it may even be remediable under other provisions of the Federal Constitution, but it is not cruel and unusual punishment. ... Surely prison was not a more congenial place in the early years of the Republic than it is today; nor were our judges and commentators so naive as to be unaware of the often-harsh conditions of prison life. Rather, they simply did not conceive of the Eighth Amendment as protecting inmates from harsh treatment. Thus, historically, the lower courts routinely rejected prisoner grievances by explaining that the courts had no role in regulating prison life."

This was in keeping with his narrow reading of the Constitution that the actions of state prison guards, no matter how brutal and reprehensible, were a matter for the states, not the federal government, to take action on.

Thomas doubled down on his rationale in a rare talk before a Black lawyer's group:

> "We took the case to decide the quite narrow issue, whether a prisoner's rights were violated under the cruel and unusual punishment clause of the Eighth Amendment as the result of a single incident of force by the prison guards which did not cause a significant injury. ... Obviously, beating prisoners is bad, but we did not take the case to answer this larger moral question."

*****

Next, there was abortion. Early on in his tenure on the court, Thomas made it clear he'd get rid of Roe the first chance he got. In one memorable case that likened abortion to eugenics, Thomas had no problem backing the majority opinion. This was a 2019 Indiana case that held that states had the right to ban abortion because it could potentially be a means of eugenics. This supposedly raised states' interest "in preventing abortion from becoming a tool of modern-day eugenics," said Thomas.

He went further, saying,

"The foundations for legalizing abortion in America were laid during the early 20th-century birth-control movement. That movement developed alongside the American eugenics movement. ... Technological advances have only heightened the eugenic potential for abortion, as abortion can now be used to eliminate concurring children with unwanted characteristics, such as a particular sex or disability. Given the potential for abortion to become a tool of eugenic manipulation, the Court will soon need to confront the constitutionality of laws like Indiana's."

Another sore point with Thomas was voting rights. He could be relied on to oppose any and every effort to strengthen voting rights laws and protections. In his view, this was another case of the federal government interfering with the right of states to decide how voting measures should be applied. Thomas quickly zeroed in on the 1965 Voting Rights Act as a prime target to make that point.

In a 1994 case, *Holder v. Hall*, he was blunt: "If one surveys the history of the Voting Rights Act, one can only be struck by the sea change that has occurred in the application and enforcement of the Act since it was passed in 1965.

"The statute was originally perceived as a remedial provision directed specifically at eradicating discriminatory practices that restricted blacks' ability to register and vote in the segregated South. Now, the Act has grown into something entirely different. ... (W)e have converted the Act into a device for regulating, rationing, and apportioning political power among racial and ethnic groups."

*****

His perennial sore point, though, was affirmative action. That was long before Thomas was ripped unmercifully by civil rights groups and his court colleague Ketanji Brown Jackson for his rabid diatribe against affirmative action in college admissions in the June 30, 2023, court strike down of affirmative action in admissions. Thomas seemed at times clinically obsessed with assailing affirmative action.

He minced no words in backing the white student plaintiff in a 2003 suit she brought against the University of Michigan law school. She claimed the school's affirmative action program discriminated against whites. Thomas cheered her on:

> "I believe blacks can achieve in every avenue of American life without the meddling of university administrators. The Constitution does not ... tolerate institutional devotion to the status quo in admissions policies when such devotion ripens into racial discrimination. .... The Law School is not looking for those students who, despite a lower LSAT score or undergraduate grade point average, will succeed in the study of law. The Law School seeks only a facade—it is sufficient that the class looks right, even if it does not perform right. The Law School tantalizes unprepared students with the promise of a University of Michigan degree and all of the opportunities that it offers."

Thomas's skewed view of the role of race in law school admissions or any other area of American life neatly conformed to his one-man crusade against efforts to expunge racial discrimination policies and practices from society. In a speech in 2020, he brusquely said that "race is a core issue" for him. It colored virtually everything he said and did on the Supreme Court.

The mix of bitterness, anger, hurt, and the clinical need for distancing that drove Thomas on racial matters came through when he wrote in his 2007 memoir,

> "I knew I'd made a mistake in going to Yale. I felt as though I'd been tricked, that some of the people who claimed to be helping me were, in fact, hurting me. ... At least Southerners were upfront about their bigotry: you knew exactly where they were coming from, just like the Georgia rattlesnakes that always let you know when they were ready to strike. Not so the paternalistic big-city whites who offered you a helping hand so long as you were careful to agree with them but slapped you down if you started acting as if you didn't know your place."

He came back to the self-imposed racial looking glass he put himself before in a speech to the mostly Black organization, the National Bar Association in 1998:

> "It pains me deeply, more deeply than any of you can imagine, to be perceived by so many members of my race as doing them harm. All the sacrifice, all the long hours of preparation were to help, not to hurt ... Isn't it time to move on? Isn't it time to realize that being angry with me solves no problems? Isn't it time to acknowledge that the problem of race has defied simple solutions and that not one of us, not a single one of us, can lay claim to the solution?"

*****

It's a mistake to think that Thomas has been solely a shill for the hardcore right, the glamour darling of ultra-conservatives, and a polarizing, extremist rightwing political and ideological gadfly. He has also been regarded by many admirers as an inspiring figure, and the source of a fount of folk wisdom about how to attain success in life. He relished that image. He has spun a number of homilies that have been oft-cited by his acolytes as glowing affirmations. Here's a sampling of Thomas's "inspirational" bromides:

"Good manners will open doors that the best education cannot."

"In my humble opinion, those who come to engage in debates of consequence, and who challenge accepted wisdom, should expect to be treated badly. Nonetheless, they must stand undaunted. That is required. And that should be expected. For it is bravery that is required to secure freedom."

"It takes a person with a mission to succeed."

"And I thank God I believe in God, or I would probably be enormously angry right now."

"The only people who have quick answers don't have the responsibility of making the decisions."

"The truth of the matter is we have become more interested in designer jeans and break dancing than we are in obligations and responsibilities."

"Daddy always seemed to be preparing for rainy days. Maybe that's why they never came."

"I began to suspect that Daddy had been right all along: the only hope I had of changing the world was to change myself first."

"An education is meaningless unless it equips students to have a better life."

"I could only choose between being an outcast and being dishonest."

The last admonition from Thomas, in which he states that he'd rather be an outcast than dishonest, was probably the most revealing. He has indeed been regarded by civil rights groups, most Blacks, and liberal Democrats as the perennial "outcast." He has plainly reveled in the role of being cast as their relentless whipping boy.

Yet, to call that a badge of honesty is a stretch. The best that can be said from this quote and the other frequently cited "inspirational" quotes from him is that his philosophy of life, the law, and public policy, like everything about him, is applauded or reviled depending on the esteem or revulsion in which he's held.

10

Shaping the Thomas Court

In February 2018, then Senate Majority Leader Mitch McConnell agreed to a sit-down interview with *Time Magazine*. There was really only one topic that McConnell wanted to talk about. That was the federal judiciary, particularly the SCOTUS. He had devoted a tremendous amount of his time, energy, and political muscle to the federal judiciary over the years.

McConnell understood what was at stake in getting rightist, ideologically rigid judges throughout the judiciary, and especially on the Supreme Court. McConnell had worked in tandem with a legion of conservative idealogues, think tanks, institutes, and major conservative corporate donors. They shared the same interest in getting a rigid conservative court.

McConnell made that goal clear to Time: "You could argue that it is my top priority, and the unique opportunity President Donald Trump has to reshape the judiciary. The impact that this Administration could have on the courts is the most long-lasting impact we could have."

Then GOP Vice Presidential candidate Mike Pence and Trump repeatedly reiterated that point during the 2016 presidential campaign. Trump, both in office and later when out of office, frequently and with great pride and pleasure reminded anyone within earshot, especially conservative groups, that he had put three Justices on the Supreme Court who fit perfectly what the ultra-right wanted and demanded to see in a SCOTUS Justice.

McConnell took special pleasure in the role he played in 2016 in torpedoing Merrick Garland, Obama's pick for the Supreme Court to replace Scalia on his death. Garland was a moderate Democrat and thus anathema to McConnell.

McConnell described exactly how and why he made sure Garland would never get on the Supreme Court: "We go into the election year in 2016. So, I sent out a statement saying that the next president would fill the nomination. So, I recommend we not have hearings, markups, anything. Because it's not about the well-qualified nominee I think we're going to get—we didn't have one yet—but it's about who ought to make the appointment. The president sent up a well-qualified nominee. My colleagues and I continued to take the position that this ought to be done by the next president."

McConnell's vow to remake the Supreme Court into an ultra-conservative bastion reflected a brutal truth. Conservatives wanted a court that would suit and complement Thomas's strict constructionist, or the coined term "originalist", concept of how the Court should decide all cases before it.

*****

Since the 1960s, the SCOTUS has been the political jewel in the crown for staunch conservatives. The court became the right's main prize during the tenure of Chief Justice Earl Warren. The right-wing routinely railed at the Warren Court for its liberal rulings upholding and expanding civil and voting rights; labor, environmental, and civil liberties protections; abortion rights; and reining in corporate abuses. These were rulings that helped not only minorities, but millions of whites in the nation to attain economic gains and expanded political and legal rights.

Conservatives railed even harder and louder at the Supreme Court as being an unapologetic advocate of activist liberalism and despised it for it. The far-right repeatedly screamed for Warren's head with signs that popped up along the highways throughout the South and the Heartland, saying, "Impeach Earl Warren."

The right wanted more Justices on the bench who would rigidly toe the ultra-conservative line. The court became even more important as a political tool for the conservative remake of the country when it became clear that just having more conservatives in the Senate and the House was not enough to roll back the gains in civil, women's, and labor rights of the past half-century.

Democrats, even when they were the minority in Congress, were on the defensive. For the most part, they were implacably hostile to conservative positions. They could, though, obstruct or outright kill the blatant anti-labor and anti-environmental protection legislation pushed by the GOP, through the filibuster.

At the same time, the nation's population and voter demographics were rapidly changing with more minorities, women, same-sex, and youth voters. Their increased vote numbers could put more spine in Democrats to stand firm against the machinations of conservatives in Congress.

The right correctly saw the Supreme Court not just as a neutral arbiter to settle legal disputes. It was a lethal weapon to skirt congressional gridlock and serve a judicial and legislative body dual role. This meant scrapping the long-standing tradition on the court whereby Justices based their legal decisions solely on the merit of the law, constitutional principles, and the public good, and not on ideology. This was a major reason Democrats made a test case of Thomas during his Senate confirmation hearings. They came up short, though, by three votes in their effort to block his confirmation.

Writer Adam Cohen traced the half-century long conservative political evolution of the SCOTUS. He noted the astounding success conservatives had in molding it into a potent legal weapon of the ultra-right to shape law and politics in the nation. He cited the musing of influential conservative lawyer Lewis Powell as a pivotal point in that evolution. In a confidential 1971 memorandum for the U.S. Chamber of Commerce, Powell posed the question: What if the major corporations could refashion the SCOTUS into a defender of capitalism and large corporations?

Powell got a chance to help answer his question when then-President Richard Nixon appointed him to the court in December 1971. With his and other subsequent appointments from GOP Presidents in the coming decades, the SCOTUS was well on the road to becoming the weapon to defend corporate interests at the expense of workers that Powell had envisioned.

*****

There are winners and losers in court decisions and rulings, like anything else in the law. The big winners with the SCOTUS rulings in the Warren Court era were workers and the poor. They were big losers in the years after.

The Warren years in the 1960s are remembered for their history-making rulings on indigent defendants' right to appointed counsel, ending the poll tax, and enhancing the rights of welfare recipients. While Blacks and Hispanics made up a disproportionate number and percentage of the poor, there were also a lot of whites who were poor, and a lot of them lived in the Midwest and South.

The conservative majority had yet another strong card to play in protecting the interests of the rich. They would claim they were not politicizing the court. Thomas repeatedly hit hard on this to deflect criticism that he was doing just that, saying, "'Judges going beyond what Article III requires and staying within the limitations on judges. There's always a temptation to go beyond," pointing to substantive due process as an example. Thomas posited this alleged politicization of the Supreme Court as "a danger" in a September,2021 lecture at Notre Dame University. By politicization, he meant liberal rulings.

Thomas's disingenuous notion of an independent court fiercely clashed with the reality of an ideologically driven court that makes decisions based on politics, not strictly the law. That ideal also clashed with the blunt truth that since the 1970s, an increasingly conservative ideologically dominant court majority has made countless decisions that blatantly violate the Constitutional precept of equal protection under the law.

Trump and his hard-right conservative backers were fully aware that the court's power to be de facto legislators could last decades. After all, presidents and congresspersons come and go, but Justices can sit there until death if they choose. Thomas's more than three decades on the court was proof of that.

Trump, Pence, and McConnell were as good as their words in getting their ideal SCOTUS Justices confirmed. They were all in the ideological image of Thomas to varying degrees. The Supreme Court had slowly evolved to become the right's protector of conservative positions on the big-ticket issues, even when those decisions harmed millions of Americans, including many of their supporters.

The GOP has long known that packing the Supreme Court with ultra-conservative Justices ensured that its decisions closely fit its ideological tenets. Thomas was the perfect example of that type of Justice.

Conclusion

"In my humble opinion, those who come to engage in debates of consequence, and who challenge accepted wisdom, should expect to be treated badly. Nonetheless, they must stand undaunted. That is required. And that should be expected. For it is bravery that is required to secure freedom."

"Perhaps some are confused because they have stereotypes of how blacks should be and I respectfully decline, as I did in my youth, to sacrifice who I am for who they think I should be."

From the moment he took his seat on the SCOTUS in October 1991, Thomas has returned again and again to variations on this theme. He has cast in stone his pariah role for many Blacks, civil rights groups, and liberal Democrats. This has been almost a badge of honor for him.

Thomas has parlayed his ideological, contrarian, ultra-right role into a lucrative, even lavish, lifestyle. Much of that can be chalked up to the gifts showered on him by ultra-conservative boosters—gifts that he has refused to disclose. His refusal violated the loose and lax disclosure law and ethics requirements of SCOTUS Justices.

Thomas's often-cited vow to outlive his liberal tormentors and get back at them has been more than just pithy, angered hyperbole. His three decades-plus stint on the SCOTUS was a testament to his staying power. During those years, he's ruled on a legion of cases.

These cases have dealt with corporate abuse and regulations, voting rights, LGBT rights, civil rights, affirmative action, abortion, environmental regulations, labor protections, immigration reforms, and the limitations on the federal government's powers to regulate and enforce protective laws for working persons. In almost every case, one could have virtually mailed his vote in. He almost always backed a conservative ruling and opposed a liberal ruling in a case.

If nothing else, this could be said about Thomas. He was one of, if not the most consistent, reliable, and predictable SCOTUS Justices that hard rightist conservatives ever had on the Supreme Court. If Thomas remained on the court through 2028, he would bag the record of being the longest-serving justice ever in SCOTUS history.

*****

Thomas voted several times to scrap race as one of the criteria for college admissions. His long game on dumping affirmative action and racial preferences in college admissions finally paid off when he and the other five conservative SCOTUS Justices rang the curtain down on it in the court's decision in June 2023. The vote was a tribute to Thomas's long and dogged opposition to racial preferences. Thomas didn't stop there. He also virtually commanded the court to revisit its rulings upholding LGBT rights, some voting rights provisions, and maybe interracial marriage.

Thomas has been endlessly denounced as being an arch-hypocrite for his stances since he arguably benefited from those same racial preferences he loathed after the fact. The criticism didn't faze him. His originalist, strict constructionist philosophy on law and public policy has been deeply encoded in his legal and judicial philosophy. This ensures that he will reflexively position himself to oppose anything that even remotely infringes on unrestricted personal and individual liberty, and property rights. His frontier, free boot capitalist, states' rights vision of America is politically, legally, and judicially non-negotiable.

The most frightening thing to Thomas's arch critics and enemies was that he seemingly had possibly many more years on the high court to continue to wreak his brand of revenge on liberal law and public policy at all levels of American society. In 2023, he was no longer a lone voice on the court. He now had the assurance that for maybe many years he would have a comfortable ultra-conservative SCOTUS majority of Justices to keep company with. Their philosophy in most cases aligned comfortably with his.

Admirers have labeled Thomas "courageous," an "inspirer," "honorable," "principled," and many more superlatives. Critics have reviled him as a "hypocrite," "sell-out," "liar," "financial grubber" and many more epithets. However, he's viewed and characterized, the one constant is that Thomas has for decades been a lightning rod for controversy. As long as Thomas is on the bench and in the public eye, that won't change.

Appendix:
The Origin of Thomas's Strict Constructionism

James Madison is often revered as the "Father of the Constitution," as he had a significant influence in the drafting of certain clauses and the ratification of the document itself. Apart from this fact, one particular debate has raged since the beginning of the Republic all the way into the present day: the debate on the way in which the Constitution of the United States should be interpreted. Many law experts have argued for a "broad" or "loose" understanding of the Constitution. Claiming it to be a "living, breathing, document," which allows for the document to evolve as American society and culture evolves. Others, however, see this view as dangerous and not what the Founders intended for the Constitution. This side, known as strict constructionism, argues that the Constitution must be read and interpreted in the manner in which it was originally written, only being able to change or evolve if absolutely necessary through a lengthy amendment process. Given the radical difference between both interpretations and that both sides claim to represent the Founders' intentions for how the supreme law of the land should be understood, it is crucial to determine which view is most correct. Therefore, given his involvement in and dedication to the Constitution, the purpose of this essay is to determine which school of interpretation James Madison practiced. To properly reach this conclusion, the contents of this essay include a summary of the methods of research utilized, an analysis of both loose and strict construction, as well as Madison's views on each, and a Biblical analysis of the issue.

The only research method conducted in the drafting of this essay was that of qualitative research. The reason for this being is that, given the theme of political thought and theory, no quantitative research was necessary or numerical data available to formulate a proper conclusion for the hypothesis. Additionally, this essay draws from and cites scholarly articles, relevant to the topic that utilizes quantitative research, as well as definitions of political terms, quotes from the Bill of Rights of the Constitution of the United States, and a passage from Scripture. The philosophical, political, and worldview-based content of these sources in addition to its lack of numerical data solidifies the utilization of them as qualitative research.

Fortunately, James Madison was an active and vocal politician, with many direct statements pertaining to the Constitution itself and his personal political philosophy. This makes the process of analyzing and determining his view on strict and loose constructionism an immensely uncomplicated process. The analysis portion of this essay initially focuses on further defining the conflicting camps of loose and strict constructionism, as well as a summary of the utilization of the Ninth and Tenth Amendments of the Constitution, which set the precedent for how the powers, enumerated in the Constitution, would be construed. After this, an analysis of Madison's actions and statements is made in order to reach a conclusion on his view of how the Constitution should be interpreted.

As stated previously, it is necessary to provide an understanding of both strict and loose constructionism to properly bind the issue faced in this essay and to better understand the arguments made. A loose constructionist is defined as "an advocate of loose construction (as of a statute or constitution)," or more specifically, "one favoring a liberal construction of the Constitution of the U.S. to give broader powers to the federal government." In an obverse manner, a strict constructionist is defined as "one who favors giving a narrow conservative construction of a given document or instrument," or once again more specifically, "one who favors a strict construction of the Constitution of the United States." The fundamental difference between loose constructionism and strict constructionism is that the former proposes an increase in the powers of the federal government, while the latter believes otherwise. Strict constructionism proposes that the Constitution must be interpreted literally and as the words were written, whereas loose constructionism warrants that the Constitution must be interpreted in a manner that gives the "implied" powers to the national government. Strict construction was the more popular of the two philosophies after the founding of the United States with early Supreme Court cases ruling in favor of it, such as *United States v. Morrison, New York v. United States, Gregory v. Ashcroft, Alden v. Maine, United States v. Lopez*, and *Printz v. United States*.

The two key amendments behind outlining the proper interpretation of the Constitution are the Ninth and Tenth Amendments. Interestingly enough, both amendments were drafted by James Madison himself. The Ninth Amendment states the following: "The enumeration in the Constitution, of certain rights, shall not be construed to deny or disparage others retained by the people." (U.S. Constitution, Amendment IX, Section I) Likewise, the Tenth Amendment states that, "The powers not delegated to the United States by the Constitution, nor prohibited by it to the states, are reserved to the states respectively, or to the people."

(U.S. Constitution, Amendment X, Section I) Of the two interpretations of the Constitution, strict constructionism finds its basis in the Tenth Amendment. In fact, the Ninth Amendment also supports strict constructionism. After the establishment of the new American republic, it was commonly understood that the Ninth Amendment actively restricted the federal government from increasing its power, while the Tenth established the principle of restriction of power, giving both a joint roll in protection against a powerful federal government.

However, the New Deal Era brought an end to the strict constructionist view of both amendments. Many of the court cases decided during Depression America were responsible for this dramatic change. The ruling of *United States v. Darby* greatly increased federal intrastate commerce powers by denying precedent that the Tenth Amendment required a strict constructionist interpretation of powers enumerated to the national government by the Constitution. Furthermore, the hearing of *Wickard v. Filburn* did not remotely acknowledge the Tenth Amendment. This change led to a major shift from the historical precedent of strict constructionist rulings based on the Ninth and Tenth Amendments to many more loose constructionist ruling in recent history.

Given a summary of strict and loose constructionism and the historical use of the Ninth and Tenth Amendments, it is imperative to analyze and determine James Madison's stance in this issue of interpretation. First and foremost, Madison believed that the federal government would fundamentally attempt to expand its powers through an improper interpretation of the Constitution. Additionally, Madison made the claim that the Constitution did not allow for the expansion of federal powers but rather solidified the powers given to it in the Articles of Confederation. In addition to this, Madison also stated:

> The powers delegated by the proposed Constitution to the federal government are few and defined. Those which are to remain in the State governments are numerous and indefinite.... The powers reserved to the several States will extend to all the objects which, in the ordinary course of affairs, concern the lives, liberties, and properties of the people, and the internal order, improvement, and prosperity of the State.

This leads to the conclusion that a broad interpretation of the Constitution leads to the misplacement of authority and power, as sovereignty belongs to the people and not the federal government. Madison also stressed the idea of veneration of the law. In fact, "Under Madisonian constitutionalism, institutions should mediate the will of the people, and constitutional change should be relatively infrequent because people need a constitution they can "venerate" and tinkering with it every generation would undermine this requirement of government." Madison disagreed with his colleague Thomas Jefferson's insistence on the will of the people regularly being reflected in the law as he believed that constantly appealing to the whims of the people would negate veneration of that same law. He believed that it would be a risk of major issues being determined by passion rather than reason. Madison was convinced of the idea of venerating the law in a similar way that one venerates Almighty God. However, despite his dedication to veneration of the law, Madison did support a process of amendment. This was due to the fact that he recognized that it was possible for a constitution to be flawed and should thus be able to be changed when necessary. Finally, Madison stressed the importance of the meaning of the language used in the law in order to prevent misinterpretation.

Having drafted both the Ninth and Tenth amendments, Madison naturally formulated opinions surrounding them. Madison interpreted both amendments as power-restraining in regard to the federal government. He also spoke out against the establishment of the national bank as a broad view of federal power and against the Ninth and Tenth Amendments. In fact, Madison's interpretation of the Ninth Amendment was utilized to promote strict constructionism by Supreme Court Justice Joseph Story. Finally, according to Madison, the purpose of the Ninth Amendment was to prevent the federal government from expanding upon the powers already enumerated to it by the Constitution.

With the analysis of Madison's given, it is possible to yield a conclusion on Madison's stance on the proper interpretation of the Constitution. Madison's political philosophy and beliefs reflected many elements of strict constructionism such as his respect and interpretation of the Constitution. Additionally, Madison's interpretation of the function of both the Ninth and Tenth Amendments was also reflective of a strict constructionist. In conclusion, it is completely logical and apparent to consider James Madison a strict constructionist.

With the necessary research conducted, it is imperative to provide a Biblical analysis of Madison's strict constructionist views. The Apostle Paul wrote the words,

> Let every person be subject to the governing authorities. For there is no authority except from God, and those that exist have been instituted by God. Therefore, whoever resists the authorities resists what God has appointed, and those who resist will incur judgment. For rulers are not a terror to good conduct, but to bad. Would you have no fear of the one who is in authority? Then do what is good, and you will receive his approval, for he is God's

servant for your good. But if you do wrong, be afraid, for he does not bear the sword in vain. For he is the servant of God, an avenger who carries out God's wrath on the wrongdoer. Therefore, one must be in subjection, not only to avoid God's wrath but also for the sake of conscience.

One of the points exhibited in this passage is respect for the law, even the laws of man. Therefore, it should be assumed that God considers obedience to the human authority and laws seriously. In addition to this, the Apostle John wrote that, "And this is love, that we walk according to his commandments; this is the commandment, just as you have heard from the beginning, so that you should walk in it." This passage reflects that obedience to God's commands is an act of love towards him. While these passages do not explicitly state that a strict constructionist interpretation and veneration of the Constitution is morally righteous, it does show that laws and commands, especially when they are from God, are to be taken seriously.

Additionally, it can be logically assumed that it is necessary to correctly understand a command or law to properly obey it.

Finally, given the extensive research exhibited, it is clear on which side of the interpretation James Madison falls. An analysis of his political beliefs points firmly towards that of Strict constructionism. Additionally, his opinions on the matter of Constitutional interpretation appear to line up Biblically. All these factors point to the principle that a proper understanding of the law and a respect of that same law are necessary for good laws to remain in existence, which is why the United States continues to be a bastion of liberty and rights to this day.

LeMay, Drew (2022) "James Madison and Strict Constructionism," *Liberty University Journal of Statesmanship & Public Policy*: Vol. 2 : Iss. 2 , Article 3. Available at: https://digitalcommons. liberty.edu/jspp/vol2/iss2/3.

Sources

Introduction

Josh Gerstein, "Clarence Thomas, Ketanji Brown Jackson air sharp disagreement on race in America," *Politico*, June 29, 2023, https://www.politico.com/news/2023/06/29/clarence-thomas-ketanji-brown-jackson-affirmative-action-00104271.

Foskett, Ken, *Judging Thomas* (New York, Harper & Collins, 2004), p. 212.

1. Above the Law

Mark Sherman, "Justice Thomas says he didn't have to disclose luxury trips," *AP*, April 7, 2023, https://apnews.com/article/supreme-court-justice-clarence-thomas-ethics-trips-2c0f59fd1b0d5d3617c1537a767c5325.

Li Zhou, "Clarence Thomas's Brazen Violation of Ethics Rules, briefly Explained," *Vox*, April 6, 2023, https://www.vox.com/politics/2023/4/6/23672921/clarence-thomas-supreme-court-propublica-luxury-trips-harlan-crow.

Joshua Kaplan, Justin Elliott and Alex Mierjeski,"Clarence Thomas Defends Undisclosed "Family Trips" With GOP Megadonor. Here Are the Facts," *ProPublica*, 4/7/April 7, 2023, https://www.propublica.org/

article/clarence-thomas-response-trips-legal-experts-harlan-crow.

Dawn Allcot, "How Rich is Clarence Thomas," *Yahoo!Finance*, October 25, 2022, https://finance.yahoo.com/news/rich-clarence-thomas-162205889.html?fr=sycsrp_catchall.

Ariane deVogue and Devan Cole, "Clarence Thomas gets extension to file financial disclosures amid scrutiny of relationship with GOP megadonor," *CNN*, July 6, 2023, https://www.cnn.com/2023/06/07/politics/clarence-thomas-financial-disclosures-supreme-court-2023/index.html.

2. Mr. "Originalist"

Charles Russell, "Clarence Thomas Describes his Judicial Philosophy, 'Get it right,'" *The Washington Free Beacon*, November 2, 2017, https://freebeacon.com/issues/clarence-thomas-describes-judicial-philosophy-get-it-right/.

Rebecca Cohen, "The Supreme Court just gutted clean water protections. Clarence Thomas suggested it didn't go far enough, *Business Insider*, May 25, 2023, https://www.businessinsider.com/supreme-court-clarence-thomas-hints-further-gut-epa-authority-2023-5.

Gregory E. Maggs, "Which Original Meaning of the Constitution Matters to Justice Thomas?" *New York Journal of Law and Liberty*, Vol., 4, 2009, http://www.law.nyu.edu/sites/default/files/ECM_PRO_064795.pdf.

Jeffrey Hicks, "The Case for Clarence Thomas, Chief Justice of the Supreme Court," New Visions Commentary, *National Center Organization*, December 1, 2004, https://nationalcenter.org/project21/2004/12/01/the-case-for-clarence-thomas-chief-justice-of-the-supreme-court-by-jeffrey-hicks/.

Ian Miillhiser, "Amy Coney Barrett's Approach to the Constitution Explained, " *Vox*, October 12, 2020, https://www.vox.com/21497317/originalism-amy-coney-barrett-constitution-supreme-court.

Scott Lemieux, "The Limits of Originalism," *The American Prospect*, April 16, 2016, https://prospect.org/article/limits-originalism/.

3. More Than His Grandfather's Son

Harold Meyerson, "How Racist are Republicans? Very," *The American Prospect*, October 22, 2020, https://prospect.org/blogs-and-newsletters/tap/how-racist-are-republicans-very/.

Simon Maloy, "CBS' 60 Minutes offered no rebuttal to Clarence Thomas' claims about Anita Hill," *Media Matters for America*, October 2, 2007, https://www.mediamatters.org/cbs/cbs-60-minutes-offered-no-rebuttal-clarence-thomas-claims-about-anita-hill.

"What Thurgood Marshall said to Clarence Thomas," *Althouse*, May 18, 2011, https://althouse.blogspot.com/2011/05/what-thurgood-marshall-said-to-clarence.html.

Earl Ofari Hutchinson, "More than his Grandfather's Son—Understanding Clarence Thomas," *The Huff Post*, October 3, 2007, https://www.huffpost.com/entry/more-than-his-grandfather_b_67039.

Ben Blanchet, "NAACP President Name-Drops Clarence Thomas In Brutal Dig Over Affirmative Action," *The Huff Post*, June 30, 2023, https://news.yahoo.com/naacp-president-name-drops-clarence-114608682.html?fr=sycsrp_catchall.

Eyder Peralta, "Supreme Court Upholds University Of Texas' Affirmative Action Program," *NPR*, June 23, 2016, https://www.npr.org/sections/thetwo-way/2016/06/23/483228011/supreme-court-upholds-university-of-texas-affirmative-action-program.

Tom Norton, "Fact Check: Did Clarence Thomas Go to Yale Under Affirmative Action Policy?" *Newsweek*, 6/30/June 30, 2023, https://www.newsweek.com/fact-check-did-clarence-thomas-go-yale-under-affirmative-action-policy-1810180.

"Clarence Thomas: Obama Only President Because He's What 'Elites' Expect 'From A Black Person' (VIDEO) | *The Huff Post*, May 3, 2013, https://www.huffpost.com/entry/clarence-thomas-obama_n_3210224.

Earl Ofari Hutchinson, "Clarence Thomas Affirmative Action's Biggest Beneficiary and Biggest Hypocrite," *The Huff Post*, August 10, 2023, https://www.huffpost.com/entry/clarence-thomas_b_3412953.

4. Obama Under Thomas's Fire

Nia Malika-Henderson, "SCOTUS to Debate Obama Citizenship," *Politico*, December 5, 2008, https://www.politico.com/story/2008/12/scotus-to-debate-obama-citizenship-016225.

Earl Ofari Hutchinson, "Method to Thomas Madness on Obama Birth Certificate," *The Huff Post*, May 11, 2011, https://www.huffpost.com/entry/method-to-thomas-madness_b_148626.

5. Thomas's Continuing Payback

Ariane deVogue, "Clarence Thomas awaits his chance to drive the conservative majority on abortion and guns," *CNN*, May 20, 2021, https://www.cnn.com/2021/05/20/politics/clarence-thomas-abortion-guns/index.html.

Matt Naham, "Famously Silent Justice Clarence Thomas stuns by Asking Questions during Oral Arguments," *Law & Crime*, May 4, 2020, https://lawandcrime.com/supreme-court/justice-clarence-thomas-stuns-by-asking-a-question-during-live-oral-arguments/.

Kimberley Strowbridge Robinson, "Clarence Thomas Wins Long Game Against Affirmative Action," *Bloomberglaw.com*, June 29, 2023, https://news.bloomberglaw.com/us-law-week/clarence-thomas-wins-long-game-against-affirmative-action.

Sonam Sheth, John L. Dorman, "Clarence Thomas isn't happy the Supreme Court went out of its

way to shoot down a fringe right-wing elections
theory," *Yahoo News*, June 27, 2023, https://
news.yahoo.com/clarence-thomas-isnt-happy-
supreme-153029400.html?fr=sycsrp_catchall.

"Clarence Thomas, 'Be Not Afraid' American
Enterprise Institute, 2001," UmbraSearch,
2001, https://www.umbrasearch.org/catalog/
e385b556ebfecd5205f1707ad02dcd55aae8f99f.

Tom Norton, "Fact Check: Was Clarence Thomas
Lone Dissenter on Trump Jan. 6 Documents?"
Newsweek, June 17, 2022, https://www.newsweek.
com/fact-check-was-clarence-thomas-lone-
dissenter-trump-jan-6-documents-1716895.

Earl Ofari Hutchinson, "Clarence Thomas's Continuing
Payback," *earlofarihutchinson.blogspot.com*,
June, 2009, https://earlofarihutchinson.blogspot.
com/2009/06/clarence-thomass-continuing-
payback.html.

6. Anita Hill's Long Shadow

"Justice Thomas in Notre Dame lecture discusses faith,
modern views," *The Catholic Sun*, September 20,
2021, https://www.catholicsun.org/2021/09/20/
justice-thomas-in-notre-dame-lecture-discusses-
faith-modern-views/.

Robert Farley, "Rep. Anthony Weiner: Law clear that
Justice Clarence Thomas must recuse himself from
health care case," *Polifact*, March 7, 2011, https://
www.politifact.com/factchecks/2011/mar/07/

anthony-weiner/rep-anthony-weiner-law-clear-clarence-thoma/.

Brian Schwartz, "Inside the consulting firm run by Ginni Thomas, wife of Supreme Court Justice Clarence Thomas," *CNBC*, April 5, 2022, https://www.cnbc.com/2022/04/05/inside-the-consulting-firm-run-by-ginni-thomas-wife-of-supreme-court-justice-clarence-thomas.html.

Josh Gerstein, "Thomas's Credibility an Issue Again," *Politico*, October 22, 2010, https://www.politico.com/story/2010/10/thomass-credibility-at-issue-again-044051.

Earl Ofari Hutchinson, "Clarence Thomas Can Breathe a Sigh of Relief with Weiner Downfall, *Op Ed News*, June 16, 2011, https://www.opednews.com/articles/Clarence-Thomas-Can-Breath-by-earl-ofari-hutchin-110616-550.html.

7. Trump's Favorite Judge

Kyle Cheney, et.al., "Trump lawyers saw Justice Thomas as 'only chance' to stop 2020 election certification," *Politico*, November 2, 2022, https://www.politico.com/news/2022/11/02/trump-lawyers-saw-justice-thomas-as-only-chance-to-stop-2020-election-certification-00064592.

Joan Biskupic, "Justice Clarence Thomas reveals some sympathy for Trump's baseless fraud claims," *CNN*, February 22, 2021, https://www.cnn.com/2021/02/22/politics/clarence-thomas-trump-election-fraud/index.html.

James Sweet, "Lessons from Clarence Thomas and Antonin Scalia's friendship," *Washington Examiner*, June 115, 2022, https://www.washingtonexaminer.com/restoring-america/fairness-justice/lessons-from-clarence-thomas-and-antonin-scalias-friendship.

Earl Ofari Hutchinson, "How About Four New Scalias On The Supreme Court," *The Huff Post*, August 1, 2017, https://www.huffpost.com/entry/how-about-four-more-scali_b_11285596.

8. Impeach Thomas?

Olafimihan Oshin, "Petition calling for Clarence Thomas removal from Supreme Court gets 1M signatures," *The Hill*, July 6, 2022, https://thehill.com/homenews/state-watch/3548012-petition-calling-for-clarence-thomas-removal-from-supreme-court-gets-1m-signatures/.

Ramsey Touchberry, "AOC calls for possible impeachment of Supreme Court justices," *The Washington Times*, July 2, 2023, https://www.washingtontimes.com/news/2023/jul/2/rep-ocasio-cortez-congress-should-consider-impeach/.

Bill Blum, "Why Clarence Thomas is a clear-cut case for impeachment from the Supreme Court," *Salon*, November 2, 2020, https://www.salon.com/2020/11/02/why-clarence-thomas-is-a-clear-cut-case-for-impeachment-from-the-supreme-court_partner/.

Earl Ofari Hutchinson, "The House is duty-bound to Bring Articles of Impeachment against Clarence Thomas," *OpEd News*, 25, 2010, https://www.opednews.com/articles/The-House-is-duty-bound-to-by-earl-ofari-hutchin-101024-749.html.

Darragh Roche, "Could Clarence Thomas Be Impeached? Legal Experts Weigh In," *Newsweek*, October 26, 2022, https://www.newsweek.com/could-clarence-thomas-impeached-legal-experts-weigh-1754785.

Stephen Neukam, "Ocasio-Cortez: 'Very difficult' to see path to impeach Clarence Thomas in GOP-led House," *CNN*, April 9, 2023, https://thehill.com/homenews/sunday-talk-shows/3941346-ocasio-cortez-very-difficult-to-see-path-to-impeach-clarence-thomas-in-gop-led-house/.

9. Clarence Thomas on Clarence Thomas

Joan Biskupic, "The quotable words of Supreme Court Justice Clarence Thomas," *CNN*, October 24, 2021, https://edition.cnn.com/2021/10/24/politics/clarence-thomas-through-the-years/index.html.

"The Top 50 Clarence Thomas Quotes (2023)," *quotefancy.com*, https://quotefancy.com/clarence-thomas-quotes.

10. Shaping the Thomas Court

Tessa Berenson, "'We'd Like to See America Right of Center.' Mitch McConnell Explains His Strategy on Judges," *Time*, 2/8/February 8, 2018, https://time.com/5138247/mitch-mcconnell-judicial-strategy/.

Paul Blumenthal, "The Supreme Court's Conservative Supermajority Continues Its Work Rolling Back The 20th Century," *The Huff Post*, 6/30/June 6, 2023, https://www.huffpost.com/entry/supreme-court-2023-term_n_649f25b7e4b030efa12065d4.

Matt Nahum, "Justice Clarence Thomas Blames Judges for Politicization of the Courts, Slams the 'Craziness' of His Confirmation Hearings, and Jokes That He Definitely 'Didn't Go Watch Hamilton," *Law & Crime*, September 17, 2021, https://lawandcrime.com/supreme-court/justice-clarence-thomas-blames-judges-for-politicization-of-the-courts-slams-the-craziness-of-his-confirmation-hearings-and-jokes-that-he-definitely-didnt-go-watch-hamilton/.

Conclusion

Dave Davies, "FRONTLINE traces the 'ambition and revenge' driving SCOTUS Justice Clarence Thomas," *NPR*, May 31, 2023, https://www.npr.org/2023/05/31/1179111708/frontline-traces-the-ambition-and-revenge-driving-scotus-justice-clarence-thomas.

Bibliography

Arkes, Hadley. *Mere Natural Law: Originalism and the Anchoring Truths of the Constitution.* Washington, DC: Regnery Gateway, 2023.

Berry, Thomas. SUMMARY AND ANALYSIS OF Amul Thapar's Book THE PEOPLE'S JUSTICE: Clarence Thomas and the Constitutional Stories that Define Him. Thomas Berry, 2023.

Biskupic, Joan. *Nine Black Robes: Inside the Supreme Court's Drive to the Right and Its Historic Consequences.* New York: William Morrow, 2023.

Foskett, Ken. *Judging Thomas.* New York: William Morrow, 2004.

Garrett, Paige Madison. *The Dissents of Clarence Thomas: Fealty to Constitutional Originalism.* Kindle Edition, 2022.

Gerber, Scott Douglas. *First Principles: The Jurisprudence of Clarence Thomas.* New York: New York University Press, 2002.

Greenhouse, Linda. *Justice on the Brink: The Death of Ruth Bader Ginsburg, the Rise of Amy Coney Barrett, and Twelve Months That Transformed the Supreme Court.* New York: Random House, 2021.

Henry, Christopher E., et al. *Clarence Thomas: Supreme Court Justice (Black Americans of Achievement)*. S.l.: n.d.

Holzer, Henry Mark. *The Supreme Court Opinions of Clarence Thomas, 1991-2011*. New York: McFarland, 2011.

Kiel, Daniel. *The Transition: Interpreting Justice from Thurgood Marshall to Clarence Thomas*. Stanford, CA: Stanford University Press, 2023)

Magnet, Myron. *Clarence Thomas and the Lost Constitution*. New York: Encounter Books, 2019.

Mayer, Jane and Jill Abramson. *Strange Justice: The Selling of Clarence Thomas*. S.l.: Graymalkin Media, 2019.

Merida, Kevin and Michael Fletcher. *Supreme Discomfort: The Divided Soul of Clarence Thomas*. New York: Crown, 2008.

Miler, Anita and Nina Totenberg. The Complete Transcripts of the Clarence Thomas - Anita Hill Hearings: October 11, 12, 13, 1991. Kindle Edition, 1991.

Pack, Michael and Mark Paoletta. *Created Equal: Clarence Thomas in His Own Words*. New York: Regnery: 2022.

Phelps, Timothy M. and Helen Winternitz. *Capitol Games: Clarence Thomas, Anita Hill, and the*

Story of a Supreme Court Nomination. New York: Hyperion, 1992.

Robin, Corey. *The Enigma of Clarence Thomas*. New York: Metropolitan Books, 2020.

Rosen, James. *Scalia: Rise to Greatness, 1936 to 1986*. Washington, DC: Regnery, 2023.

Tang, Aaron. *Supreme Hubris: How Overconfidence Is Destroying the Court—and How We Can Fix It*. New Haven, CT: Yale University Press, 2023.

Thapar, Amul. *The People's Justice: Clarence Thomas and the Constitutional Stories that Define Him*. Washington, DC: Regnery Gateway, 2023.

Thomas, Andrew Peyton. *Clarence Thomas: A Biography*. San Francisco, CA: Encounter Books, 2001.

Thomas, Clarence. *My Grandfather's Son: A Memoir*. New York: Harper Perennial, 2008.

———. *Clarence Thomas: Confronting the Future: Selections from the Senate Confirmation Hearings and Prior Speeches*. New York: Gateway, 1992.

Toobin, Jeffrey. *The Nine: Inside the Secret World of the Supreme Court*. New York: Anchor Books, 2008.

Waldman, Michael. *The Supermajority: How the Supreme Court Divided America*. New York: Simon & Schuster, 2023.

Whitehorse, Sheldon and Jennifer Mueller. *The Scheme: How the Right Wing Used Dark Money to Capture the Supreme Court*. New York: The New Press, 2022.

Whitehorse, Dan. *Clarence Thomas Biography: Rising Above Adversity*. Dan Whitehorse, 2023.

Woodward, Bob and Scott Armstrong. *The Brethren: Inside the Supreme Court*. New York: Simon & Schuster, 2005.

About the Author

Earl Ofari Hutchinson is the author of multiple books on race and politics in America. He is a political analyst and has appeared on MSNBC and on CNN. His books include the trilogy on the *Obama Years: The Obama Legacy*; *How Obama Governed: The Year of Crisis and Challenge*; and *How Obama Won*. His most recent books are *The Trump Challenge to Black America; From King to Obama: Witness to a Turbulent History*; and *Bring Back the Poll Tax— The GOP War on Voting Rights*.

Index

Warren Court, 68, 70

Warren, Earl, 68-9

Watergate, 55

Weiner, Anthony, 41-3, 45

whites, 18, 19, 26, 62-3, 69, 71

Wickard v. Filburn, 80

Wisconsin, 48

Wright, Angela, 55

Yale Law School, 24-5

9 7 9 8 8 9 1 2 1 1 7 3 5